BE A LOCAL COUNCILLOR

A Practical Guide to Representing
Your Community

Peter Arnold

How To Books

Acknowledgement
Certain forms in this book are reproduced by kind permission of the
publishers Shaw & Sons Ltd of 21 Bourne Park, Bourne Road, Crayford,
Kent DA1 4BZ, from whom supplies may be obtained.

First published in 1992 by How To Books Ltd, Plymbridge House,
Estover Road, Plymouth PL6 7PZ, United Kingdom.
Tel: Plymouth (0752) 705251. Fax: (0752) 695699. Telex: 45635.

Typeset by Concept Communications Ltd, Crayford, Kent.

Printed and bound by The Cromwell Press Limited, Melksham, Wiltshire

Contents

Preface

At the time this book was under consideration, it was fairly easy to define the various areas of local government: to describe the functions of County Councils, Metropolitan Borough Councils, District Councils, Parish Councils and Neighbourhood Councils. However, the whole thing is now in the melting pot for the second time in two decades.

Early in 1991, the Secretary of State for the Environment announced a root-and-branch review of local government, and things will certainly change during the lifetime of the book. However, it is perfectly possible to describe the functions of a local Councillor, and to give practical advice on many aspects of election, and of doing the job once elected. Indeed, if past experience is any guide, a new structure for local government will produce a whole new crop of people wishing to stand for election.

There has been a long tradition of male chauvinism in local government, with terms such as chairman and mayor expressed in the masculine gender. At times in this book the male pronoun has been used for convenience and no sexism is intended. For the future there is no reason why women and men in local government should not evolve a language and terminology more suited to the needs of modern society.

How to Be a Local Councillor has been produced very much with an eye to the future. The information it contains should be sound, whatever the future holds for that peculiarly British institution, the local council.

Peter Arnold

Loganbury City Council

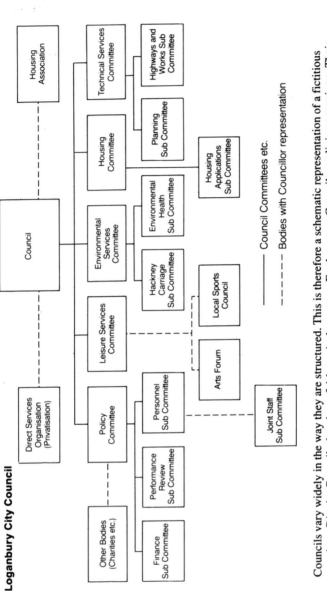

Councils vary widely in the way they are structured. This is therefore a schematic representation of a fictitious non-unitary District Council, showing a fairly typical structure. Furthermore, Councils are living organisms. Their structures evolve according to changing circumstances, including Government legislation. WorkingParties are set up, flourish and wither when their purpose is achieved. An aspiring Councillor doesn't have to know the structure in detail before election, but it is as well to have some idea of how things work.

1
Do You Really Want to be a Local Councillor?

Ask any local councillor why he took the job on in the first place, and you'll probably get one or more from a variety of answers:

'I wanted to help the community.'
'I wanted to support my political party.'
'There were issues I felt strongly about.'
'I'm interested in planning/housing/the environment.'
'I thought I could do better than the bunch of knotheads there already.'

Very common, is that last one, even if phrased more politely. All of the answers quoted are perfectly cogent reasons for wanting to become a member of a local authority, but when you really come right down to it, most councillors first exposed themselves to the trauma of a local election simply because someone asked them to.

It may surprise you to learn that there isn't actually a queue of people waiting to stand for election. Most political associations, and other groups seeking representation at council level, have periods when they are, quite frankly, scratching around for suitable candidates.

This is particularly true when the shades of opinion they represent are unpopular. It wasn't much fun, for example, being a conservative candidate in spring 1990, just after the Poll Tax was introduced. Even at the best of times, however, it isn't easy to find people to stand for election who have a reasonable chance of winning the seat.

Consequently, most organisations are constantly keeping an eye open for likely material. Suitable candidates are found from a variety of sources:

- members of ward committees

- people met during the course of political activity

- people whose circumstances have changed, so that they can now afford the time (retirement, change of job, children grown up etc)

- New arrivals in the area

Even so, there are always far more people who would make good councillors, than there are those willing to do the job.

There are also many people to whom the idea has never occurred, and need time to consider.

Of course, there are those – political activists, most commonly – who sincerely *do* want to hold a seat on the local council. They don't have a decision to make, and their only problem is to get their colleagues to see things their way. *Those* people won't be either deterred or encouraged by anything said in this book, but will find useful information here.

It's impossible to give a complete description of local government procedures and practices in an introductory book like this. Parish councils, neighbourhood councils, district councils, city councils, county councils, metropolitan borough councils – all differ in responsibilities and methods of operation.

Even between two local authorities in the same tier of government, there can be considerable variation. Here's an example:

Environmental health
Markets
Cemeteries and crematoria
Licensing
Hackney carriages

All these important functions are responsibilities of a district council. In many cases, all are controlled by one 'Environmental Services Department', with one committee overseeing the lot. Sometimes, however, things are different.

Markets may have a committee of their own. Cemeteries and Crematoria may well, oddly enough, be the responsibility of a Leisure and Recreation Committee, because that's the outfit which looks after open green spaces, Licensing may be split between several committees, and Hackney Carriages seen as a function of a Highways Committee.

To cover all possible variations would be encyclopaedic. But it *is* possible to tell you what a local councillor actually does, and –

to start with – help you make the primary decision: Do you really want to be a local councillor?

THE DECISION TO STAND

Here's a list of factors – probably only partial, but at least it will get you thinking the right way:

Your time
Your job
Your family
Your health
Your articulacy
Your financial situation
Your skin – how thick is it? ?

Take each of these factors, and jot down how you think membership of your local council will affect it – or be affected by it. The mere act of writing your thoughts down, in this way, will structure your thinking. It will help you come to a fairly dispassionate decision, eliminating your understandable euphoria at the idea as far as possible. Here are some thoughts on the matter.

Your time

'If you want something done, ask a busy man', goes the old saying. There's a great deal of truth in it, because 'a busy man' is usually the sort of chap who makes sure he's active all the time, whatever he's doing.

Make no mistake about it – membership of a local authority is a time consuming occupation. You can't treat it the way you would your golf club or your townswomen's guild.

Let's assume you're a fairly average local councillor, with no chairmanships or other extra responsibilities. Council committees usually operate on a cycle of about six weeks, followed by full Council. There is probably a group meeting of some sort towards the end of the period. That's the meeting where your own political or other grouping gets together to plan tactics for full Council. That averages about one meeting a week. Doesn't sound too bad, does it?

But things aren't quite as simple as that. To start with, meetings aren't usually spaced out regularly throughout the cycle. You may find you have three meetings in one week, and nothing the week after.

This is counteracted to some extent by the fact that you know the dates of meetings up to a year in advance, and can plan accordingly, but there is always the chance of special or *ad hoc* meetings called to discuss some particular issue.

The standard committee and council meetings are by no means, however, the whole story. Many local organisations will have council representation on their executive committees – law centres, Community Health Councils and Citizens Advice Bureaux are good examples. You may well find yourself drafted on to such bodies, and the trap in that is that you'll find that you're invited to fill such spots precisely because you have special knowledge or interest in the subject in question, and find it difficult to refuse.

You'll also find that you are invited to join different organisations simply because the people concerned think it would be useful to have a councillor among their number.

You know the sort of thing – 'Old George was a good cricketer in his time. He'd be very handy when we're after a grant for our new pavilion'! Again, such invitations are often hard to refuse and, in any case, are very useful electorally.

Neither must you underestimate the time which constituency work takes. You'll probably need to attend local ward committee meetings, and take a full part in social and fund-raising efforts.

That's when your dignity as a local councillor can go by the board. Not so long ago, in a village in Gloucestershire, the reigning Mayor and an Air Vice Marshal could be seen sharing the 'sticking up' duties at a skittle match – not, you may feel, exactly the image of a senior civic and a high-ranking serving officer.

And don't forget that you must always be available to your constituents. Remember that a person with a problem doesn't have to approach his own ward councillor with it. Any member of the appropriate authority has an obligation to help if he or she can. To be fair, many local councillors tend to overstate the time this takes, which can, in any case, be shortened by experience, but it's an important consideration, nevertheless.

Then there's the other sort of time factor. Full Council can take up to twelve hours, especially at budget time. Obviously, there are breaks for refreshment, and it's perfectly possible to nip out of the council chamber for a breather now and then (as long as you don't miss a vote), but stamina can play a part. If you're tired, you don't operate as effectively as you might.

Don't forget, however, thousands of men and women, often with families and nine-to-five jobs, *do* manage to live full and satisfying lives while being councillors. Don't let the time factor alone put you off.

The effect on your job

You can't let your council membership get in the way of earning your living, and in theory, it shouldn't do anything of the sort. But there are practicalities to consider.

Working for someone else

If you work for someone else, especially in a small business, you won't want to cause problems for your employer, who may well worry about the time you may have to take off from work, or the number of occasions when you will need to leave early to attend meetings.

The law says that employers must allow employees reasonable time off to discharge duties as a Member of a local authority, and most large organisations have developed rules and systems accordingly. Often, a councillor is allowed a set number of days for the purpose, and after that is used up, has to take annual leave.

So far, so good, but attitudes differ enormously. Many employers rather like the idea of having a councillor on their books, believing it confers a measure of prestige on the company, and that it may yield some advantage in any dealings they may have with their local authority.

On the other hand, there are those who simply see a decrease in the amount of work they're going to get out of one particular pair of hands. They can't actually do anything about it, but life can get difficult if promotion is in the air, or the time comes when you have to ask for a rise.

Working for yourself

The decision to stand for election may be complicated if you are self employed. The ability to tailor your working hours to suit can be a tremendous advantage, but on the other hand, you have to consider whether your business can afford your absence for any significant amount of time.

When considering this aspect, you should certainly find out just when council meetings are held. County councils tend to hold a high proportion of their meetings during the day, while Districts concentrate on the evenings.

Nevertheless, there are going to be daytime meetings. Members on personnel committees, for example, will be involved in meetings with trades union representatives, and as unions are entitled to use working time for their activities, such get-togethers are almost invariably held during the day.

The effect on your family

A male councillor doesn't see so much of his family as 'normal' members of the public do. If you have school-age children then perhaps you won't be willing to risk missing school plays, family outings and similar activities.

A mother of such children finds life much more difficult, and this is one of the major reasons why we don't have as many lady councillors as we should. This is a pity, because ladies with first-hand, current experience in bringing up children are a priceless asset to a local authority.

A move towards providing creches for lady members' children is slowly gathering momentum, but such a system will always be less than ideal.

Don't forget the social and civic dimension either. Membership of a local authority can certainly enrich your social life no end, but it might mean you spend more money on baby sitters.

Problems don't go away entirely when children get older, either. Teenagers tend to be acutely embarrassed by prominent parents, and simply don't want to know.

Spare a thought for your partner, too. There will be more sitting at home alone, which might not go down too well. On the other hand, he or she will get involved in some very interesting activities, not usually available to everyone. Think about royal visits, for example . . .

Health factors

Council work can be stressful. There will be times when you find yourself acutely unpopular. There are other times when the level of activity is high, and you get home late, just wanting to fall into bed, but unable to sleep when you get there, because the events of the last few hours keep revolving in your head.

If you have any reason to believe that this is likely to give you problems, then go and see your doctor, and get some advice. In any case, regular medical checks aren't a bad idea, however fit you are.

Most councils go to considerable lengths to ensure that people with physical handicaps aren't precluded from membership. Wheelchair access is usually provided, but not inevitably. There are quite a number of blind councillors doing a perfectly good job.

Give thought to any regular medication you may be taking. In fact, make sure you can take it. The odd pill or so isn't a problem, but a diabetic, for example, might have difficulty with self-injection in the middle of a meeting which has gone on for longer than expected.

Are you articulate?
The 'gift of the gab' certainly helps. But you shouldn't be put off if you don't have it. A logically-presented case, quietly and sincerely expressed, can be much more effective than flights of electric oratory. Time spent 'doing your homework' will pay more dividends than verbal pyrotechnics.

Think of Sir Geoffrey Howe's merciless demolition of Mrs Thatcher in the House of Commons, leading to her eventual resignation, if you want an example – and then remember what happened to Michael Heseltine in the ensuing leadership election, for all his admirable qualities of eloquence.

Obviously, you will be asked to get up on your hind legs and spout, but the councillor who is on his feet every five minutes often commands less attention than the one whose contributions are less frequent, but more considered.

Perhaps you're nervous about speaking in public: most people are. But you'll find that those nerves rapidly disappear, once you've got your feet wet.

In any case, there's far more to council work than addressing meetings. Face to face conversation with fellow members, officers and members of the public is quite probably more important.

If you're the sort of person who can't string two words together without 'Ums', 'Ers', 'Y' Knows' and expletives, then you probably won't get nominated for council anyway, so the question won't arise.

Your financial situation
Don't make any mistake – council membership is likely to cost you money. The old attendance allowance system which paid councillors according to the number of meetings they attended, has been replaced by a lump-sum system, with extra payments for special responsibilities, but these vary widely, and neither arrangement ever allowed anyone to make money from their membership, whatever you may read in the tabloid press.

Those payments are intended to defray costs necessarily incurred by councillors. They contribute to telephone bills and similar outgoings, but other expenses arise in unexpected ways.

When a councillor goes to some social event, he'll probably buy more raffle tickets than most people. You'll be asked to attend more dances, dinners and the rest than you're used to. You'll probably find yourself buying more clothes than you would have otherwise.

It wouldn't be right to over-emphasise this point, but it's a consideration, nevertheless.

Your skin – how thick is it?

Any councillor, who is doing the job properly, will come under attack from time to time. There is always someone who takes an opposing view to you and won't be slow in making that fact abundantly clear.

It's impossible to be all things to everyone, and still be an effective Member. All you can do is do the job the way you see it, and be prepared to take the consequences.

Sometimes, the attacks can become personal, reflecting on your competence or even your life style and family circumstances, and as the art of gentlemanly insult now seems virtually dead, they can be crude and hurtful.

When your council chamber opponents attack you, at least they will do so in full knowledge of the facts of the issue in question. People who write to local newspapers, chaps you come across in the local pub and others from the general public often don't have all the facts at their fingertips, and quite frankly, don't want to know. It can be infuriating to be attacked from a standpoint of invincible ignorance.

All councillors get used to this, and rapidly learn to shrug things off, or give as good as they get, but a new and inexperienced member can have a rough ride to start with.

Are you willing to take an ego-bruising?

Testing the water

All the above factors have, quite deliberately, been painted in fairly black colours. Things really aren't as bad as all that, and there's a great deal of pleasure and satisfaction to be had from council membership.

It's no bad thing to consider the worst scenario at this point. Having done that, attend one or two council and committee meetings – the vast majority are open to the public – and see if they provide a scene you would like to be in.

Then talk to one or two sitting councillors, and get them to clear any points you may like to raise. You'll find they will be glad to give you the benefit of their experience.

WHAT SORT OF PEOPLE BECOME LOCAL COUNCILLORS?

Just about anyone, really. It's one of the strengths of the system, providing a genuine cross-section of opinion, age groups, income brackets, ethnic origins, family backgrounds and life styles.

In the council chamber, a council tenant has just as many votes, and just as much opportunity to make his views known, as a landed aristocrat. The comprehensive school product is as equally regarded as the Old Etonian.

There are some exceptions. Lunatics, convicts and undischarged bankrupts are barred from membership. Local government officers can't become members of the authority for which they work. Indeed, fairly recent legislation has also deprived officers over a certain level of seniority of the right to sit on *any* local authority, whether it's the one which employs them or not.

The days when council work was the prerogative of the gentry and the rich are long gone. So don't think 'It's not for the likes of me'. It is.

PERSONAL QUALITIES

Reaching decisions

Obviously, councillors are expected to be honest, trustworthy and hardworking. Quite apart from that, however, one very important quality you must have is the ability to make a decision. And that's not as common as all that.

Rights and wrongs of a matter can often be very evenly balanced, but a decision has to be made – and made within a short period of time. Furthermore, there are many occasions when that decision cannot be reversed, so you only get one chance to get it right.

Example: deciding a planning question
Here's an example, based on fact. What would you do? Think your way through the problem, and decide on what course of action you would take.

Your borough has a housing problem. In one street there is a group of six houses which have been declared unfit for habitation. A private developer has acquired the site, and made a planning application to demolish, and replace them with twelve low-cost dwellings, suitable for small families. A group of squatters has moved in, and refuse to move of their own volition. Small children are involved.

Question
Do you:

- Grant planning permission, knowing that this will result in eviction of the squatters? As the housing authority, you are responsible for housing homeless people, which will probably mean bed-and-breakfast accommodation, possibly for years. You are also conscious, however, that your borough will, in the end, have six more units of family accommodation than it did before.

- Grant planning permission, while rehousing the squatters as family accommodation becomes available? This means, however, that the squatters will have jumped the housing queue, to the detriment of families who have been on your housing list for years. But you will still get your twelve dwellings, and have avoided emotive headlines and possibly TV coverage.

The third alternative would be to refuse planning permission, but this is probably not viable, because the developer would probably win an appeal to the Secretary of State for the Environment. While this would have the same end result as the first response, the process would be expensive and time-consuming. You would have lost the goodwill of the developer.

Even if the authority won the Appeal, you would still be left with families living in sub-standard conditions, and would lose valuable units of accommodation.

Do you feel confident that you could make such decisions, not occasionally, but as a matter of routine?

There is a great deal to be said for seeing all sides of a question, but eventually you will have to come down off the fence – and then live with the consequences of your decision.

Other qualities required
The ability to think on your feet is also valuable. There isn't always time – in the middle of a debate, for example – to consult with colleagues and officers.

Other useful qualities are:

- the ability to pick the essential bones from a mass of technical information;

- the ability to suffer fools gladly;

- the ability to *listen.*

Perhaps Polonius in *Hamlet* gave the best advice: 'To thine own self be true, thou canst not then be false to any man'.

EFFECTS ON YOUR FAMILY

The impact that your council membership may have on your family has been touched upon earlier, but there are one or two more points worth making.

As a local councillor, you will invariably find yourself living in something of a goldfish bowl. The same can be said, to a lesser extent, of the members of your immediate family.

For example, if your son is found guilty of a relatively minor driving offence it will probably attract local press headlines of the order of COUNCILLOR'S SON FINED FOR SPEEDING, rather than just the usual bald statement on the court reports page.

You'll also discover that friends and acquaintances of family members use that relationship to get to you: 'Hey! Your Dad's a Councillor. Can't he help?'

That's not necessarily a bad thing, but the kids might get a little tired of it.

On the other hand, there are quite welcome spin-offs too. Councillors' wives probably get taken out more often than most, and could well acquire a better wardrobe.

To a certain extent, council membership is a family affair, and it wouldn't be wise to treat it in any other light.

IT'S A WAY OF LIFE

What *is* council membership anyway? It can't really be called a job, and it isn't just a hobby. Once you've been elected, your life will never be the same again.

Even your thinking changes. Drive through a strange town and notice an ugly building; you probably don't say 'What a monstrosity!' Your reaction is more likely to be 'How did they get planning consent for *that*?'

If you're a member of an Environmental Health Committee, you can't visit a restaurant without wondering what the kitchens are like.

You'll also find that you acquire the wettest shoulder in your area, because so many people insist on crying on it.

It doesn't matter what the problem is: marital, financial, legal or whatever, perhaps completely unrelated to Council affairs, the local Councillor tends to become the repository of all tribulations.

Fortunately, the answer is often quite simple. People probably know perfectly well what the answer is, and all you have to do is listen sympathetically and allow them to talk themselves into it, which is a very valuable service to perform for anyone.

On the other hand, as a local councillor, you do get to know a great many people, and if you yourself can't help, you can probably point the sufferer towards someone who can.

Council membership is a way of life. It's satisfying, infuriating, stimulating, boring, sometimes even comic.

And it's a marvellous experience, not given to everyone to undergo.

2
A Councillor's Commitments

At this point, it would be as well to be absolutely sure of just what you're getting yourself into. There's no denying that a councillor's life is not the same as that of an 'ordinary' member of the public, and you'd better get used to that fact from day one.

Details vary from area to area, and from council to council, but the following notes won't be far wrong, wherever you live.

YOUR COMMITMENTS IN THE WARD

The local party

The vast majority of local councillors are members of one or other of the major national political parties, who have helped them get elected – spending money in the process – and have local ward organisations to whom the council member reports.

This is not invariably true, of course. Organisations such as residents associations run a similar system in some places, for example. And there are such things as completely Independent Councillors, who don't report to anyone, except their electorate.

That's the theory, anyway, but even independents have their political beliefs, and usually align themselves with a political grouping on the council. One very experienced Conservative Councillor puts it this way:

'Voting for me is like drinking keg bitter. It mightn't be precisely to your taste, but at least you know what you're getting. That isn't always true of an independent.'

Ward committee meetings typically take place once a month, and you'll be expected to attend regularly, and probably report on your doings since the last meeting. The committee will also expect you to take action on local problems which have arisen.

It's not all council work, however. A frequent complaint amongst Councillors is that such committees seem to spend more time on fund raising than they do on politics, and you'll be expected to give a hand in organising events, selling raffle tickets, manning jumble sales, going on coach trips, and all the rest.

The local committee is your power base, and you ignore that fact at your peril.

Being under the microscope

A councillor usually finds that it takes longer to do the shopping than it does other people. That's because people like him, or her, to stop and chat. And that's not just people who have problems. Anyone is entitled to an opinion on any matter, and is perfectly entitled to bend the councillor's ear on the matter.

This isn't at all a bad thing. If you are accustomed, for example, to visiting your local community centre, then it's a good idea to make sure you're there at the same time every week. People will soon get to know where to find you, and will often say things to you that they don't like to bother you with at home. You can rapidly find yourself running an informal 'surgery'.

The old saying goes: 'More know Tom Fool than Tom Fool knows', and this is particularly true of local councillors. You'll find yourself being addressed by your Christian name by people you barely know by sight. If you're doing your job properly, just about everyone in the Ward will soon know perfectly well who you are. You can't be a private sort of person and a local councillor.

Relationships with friends and business contacts

This can be a difficult area. It's all very well to say 'Such things shouldn't influence me at all', but inevitably they do.

If a close friend or relative has a problem, you wouldn't be human if you didn't pull the stops out to try and solve it. If it's someone you work with, or see every day, the situation becomes even more difficult.

The point comes where you just have to say 'Sorry – I can't help any more', and if that loses you a friend, so be it. Conversely, there's no better way of losing a friend than putting him under an obligation to you. One useful solution is to ask a fellow councillor to handle the problem for you.

Business contacts can be even trickier. Someone who puts a lot of work your way is very hard to refuse, and again, probably the best thing to do is to ask another Member to help.

Approaches are seldom as crude as 'Can you get that council contract for me?', and if you are simply asked for advice on such matters, or asked who the proper council officer is to approach, and how to set about it, then there's nothing wrong with helping where you can. After all, you have a duty to your local business community as well as to individuals.

You can very easily find yourself in the situation of having to declare a financial or personal interest at council or committee meetings, which isn't really a problem, but can deprive your council group of your vote or your contribution to debate. More about this aspect later.

This is a very grey area, but you should be prepared to deal with it if you are to serve on your local authority.

Making yourself available

A councillor must be readily available to his constituents at all times. You should not, for example, allow your telephone to go 'ex directory' if you can possibly avoid it. People must know where to find you, in a hurry. If necessary, you should consider holding local surgeries, and you must be prepared to visit the council offices at reasonably short notice.

This high profile goes with the job, and there's no acceptable way to avoid it.

Problems of individuals

You are committing yourself to helping individuals solve their problems. More – you can't avoid listening to people with problems, whether they have anything to do with your Council or not. This is time-consuming, and can be harrowing.

Again, there's no way to avoid this, even if you want to. Remember, nothing gets around an area faster than the remark 'I went to old so-and-so and he didn't do a blessed thing.' You can't help everyone, but you are obliged to try.

Building up your local knowledge

Local councillors are supposed to know everything – and that is especially true of events in your local ward. If an anonymous group of chaps come along and start digging up the road, then you are expected to know the authority concerned, what they are doing, and how long they're going to take about it. On the other hand, if a road needs digging up, you are supposed to know when the job will be done.

If something happens in your area, and you don't know what it's all about, then it's up to you to find out – and you have the contacts to do just that. Briefly, you are committing yourself to having your finger on the pulse at all times, which can be a chore, but can be extremely interesting, too.

YOUR COMMITMENTS IN THE COUNCIL CHAMBER

The council cycle

Typically, a council operates on a six-week cycle – a round of programme committee meetings, followed by full Council. There is usually a recess in August, and you may find that, if you're not going to miss meetings, then that's the time you may have to take your holidays, which is the expensive part of the year.

In addition, there are almost invariably special meetings called to discuss an urgent or vital matter, and they can crop up at any time, but are inclined to become more frequent when you approach budget time, when the level of Poll Tax or Council Tax is set.

This is probably the aspect of the business which occurred to you in the first place, and obviously, the more committees you sit on, the more onerous the duty becomes.

Attendance at meetings

You can't skip meetings. Of course – you may fall ill, or some overriding circumstance arises which precludes your attendance occasionally, and everyone understands that, but the perpetual round of meetings is probably the most onerous part of a councillor's work.

There are sanctions to make sure you do attend. In the ultimate, an absence of six months from council or committee can result in your being deprived of your seat, but long before that stage arrives, you'll find that your group leader will be hauling you over the coals for your lack of effort. And that is never forgotten when plum jobs become vacant.

The time it takes

One can always be wrong about the length of time a meeting is going to take. An agenda of thirty items can be over in an hour or so, but one with only half a dozen items can sometimes last for hours.

The only safe thing to do is write off the evening (or afternoon) of a meeting for any other purpose, although experience will teach you how long any particular gathering is likely to take.

Never be tempted to tell your partner that you'll be home at such-and-such a time. It's all Lombard Street to a china orange that that is just the occasion when you're held up for hours.

Reading time

People new to the field rarely take into account how much time sheer reading takes. You'll find that few days elapse without a council envelope coming through your letter box, and you have to assimilate every one of them, even if they relate to committees on which you do not serve.

Some councillors allocate specific times of the day or week for this purpose, others find that travelling by public transport yields very useful reading time.

Council minutes and agendas aren't the most rivetting of literature, but they do have to be read.

Extra responsibilities

When you get to the stage where you take on extra responsibilities – committee chairs for example – then your available time for anything else shrinks accordingly. Some chief officers of council departments like to talk to their chairperson on a daily basis, which does have the advantage of keeping you well informed. Others like to have a regular weekly meeting.

However you organise your committee, you'll find that the number of meetings you attend proliferates. Meetings with other chairs, with officers . . . they all take time.

IN THE COUNCIL OFFICES

Your relationships with council officers

You won't get far as a local councillor unless you are on good terms with the paid officers of the council. You can't get to know all of them, of course, but you can acquaint yourself with those in strategic positions, and these would include the Chief Executive and the Chief Officers of the various departments and their immediate deputies.

They also include people much further down the ladder. The person who is responsible for maintaining street lamps, for example, can save you a great deal of time and paperwork. So can the progress clerk in the Works Department.

Contrary to popular mythology, council officers aren't unfeeling bureaucrats who drop everything for a cup of tea, and insist on having everything signed in quintuplicate. Usually, they're perfectly normal people who are simply trying to get on with their job.

Storming around and giving orders doesn't endear you to anyone. As the old saying goes, 'you catch more flies with treacle than with vinegar'. There's no point in throwing your weight around and making a drama out of a problem unless you absolutely have to.

Similarly, councillors who dash off letters to officers every day, when a simple phone call will do the job, simply invoke the 'crying wolf' syndrome. Much better to reserve your big guns until you really need them. Then everyone will know you're serious.

Doing everything by the book takes less time than getting on good terms with everyone. But you achieve less too. And you're committed to doing the best job you can for your constituents – whatever it takes.

The demand for immediate reactions

If someone has a problem, he wants you to solve it *now* and dropping into the appropriate office next time you're passing usually isn't good enough. You need to set up your own system to allow you to respond to an enquiry quickly. This means that reacting to a request takes priority over your own personal concerns. It can be inconvenient and downright annoying, but it can give you a lot of satisfaction, too.

Finding your way around the council offices

Even though there is a trend towards centralisation, most local authorities have premises scattered around their area, and you need to know who does what, and where their offices are. This means that you have to be prepared to visit several sites when the need arises.

This isn't usually so much of a problem in compact, urban authorities, but the mileage involved when you're a Member of a rural authority can be considerable. The ability to travel around your authority's area is a significant consideration.

YOUR COMMITMENT TO A POLITICAL GROUP

If you are seeking election with the help and support – quite possibly, financial – of a political or other organisation, then you owe them your allegiance once you have won your seat. This involves being a member of that organisation's **group** on the council. This doesn't mean that you're just a 'party hack', or sheer vote fodder, but it does impose certain restraints on you.

Group meetings

Every group will hold a meeting, usually on council premises, before each full council. This is the occasion when all the committee minutes of the preceding cycle are considered, and strategy and tactics worked out for the forthcoming council meeting. No councillor can know everything about everything, and you will be briefed about topics which aren't in your immediate sphere of interest, and be able to seek explanations about things which aren't immediately clear to you.

It is also your opportunity to raise any matter you think worth airing at council. If your colleagues agree, you're in business.

However, it's a very fortunate group which doesn't have to meet more often than once a cycle. In the period immediately before the council's budget meeting, when the level of Poll Tax is set, for example, it can seem as if you are living in the council offices.

Group meetings are vital. You can't skip them however you happen to be feeling that evening.

Group decisions

You will be expected to abide by decisions reached at group meetings, and speak and vote accordingly. This is not, however, quite such a strait jacket as it may appear at first sight. After all, you will have had a hand in making those decisions.

There will be occasions when you disagree with the decisions taken, for a variety of reasons. Sometimes, a proposed course of action which is good for your local authority may not be so good for your ward – the planned line for a new road, for example, may intrude on a piece of green space in your area which you wish to preserve.

Your group will understand that, and will try to resolve your dilemma for you. If that proves impossible, then you may be allowed to abstain from voting on that topic, with no hard feelings.

Most of the time, you will agree with your group because you are of the same political persuasion as them, and see things the same way. On the occasion when you feel you can't agree, you will usually find that there is time to reach some compromise. If that's not so, then you may be tempted to abstain at the forthcoming meeting. Only on very few occasions will you find yourself voting against your group.

Only if you are a complete independent – and many of those are members of one group or another – will you not be obliged to accept group discipline.

The party whip

You'll hear, and probably read, a lot of nonsense about this topic. A **whip**, in this context, is a decision reached by a group which compels all members to vote in a particular way, and no good group leader wants to impose such a constraint unless he positively has to. Furthermore, he, or she, won't impose a whip without the overwhelming consent of the majority of group members.

In practice, very few whips are imposed by most groups: whole years can go by without a single example. It is certainly not something which should frighten you in any way at all.

However, whips *are* imposed by groups on infrequent occasions, and you have to accept that fact.

Working with the opposition

Opposition council members don't have two heads and eat babies for breakfast. Some of them are quite nice, really. And you're going to have to work with them.

The most obvious example of this is the 'hung council' situation, where no one group has overall control. In that situation, you'll have to co-operate with at least one other group to get any council business done at all. You may find that your group has to compromise, on occasion, in order to achieve their goals.

It's also worth remembering that much – some would say 'most' – council business has precious little to do with politics, and that decisions can be reached without disagreement.

You can also find yourself working with the opposition when you belong to one political party, and other councillors in your ward represent another. In those circumstances, it obviously makes sense to close ranks against the outside world, when you can, to get something done for your own constituents.

So you must be prepared to work with some unexpected people from time to time. After all, you don't have to like a person to work with him.

PREPARING YOURSELF

If you decide to stand for election, you'd better be prepared to be beaten.

Indeed, if your opponent is a respected sitting councillor, then the chances are that you are batting on a sticky wicket from day one.

But there's never anything inevitable about such situations. The national political climate, like it or not, has a profound effect, and there are many examples of well-known and popular local personalities beating highly experienced councillors at a first attempt.

On the other hand, if you stand for election, you'd better be prepared to *win*. Most people, first time around, think to themselves, 'Who, in their right mind, is going to vote for me?', but you'll be surprised.

If you're a political nominee, then you can count on the hard core of your party's supporters. You can also hope for the mass of voters who don't take an active part in politics, perhaps never think about the subject very much, but, as a matter of course, always cast their vote for your party.

Remember, well under half of the electorate bother to vote at local elections. This is a highly regrettable fact, but one which enables you to define your potential vote fairly closely. You can assume that the 'faithful' of all parties will turn out, and there's nothing anyone can do to get them to switch their votes. It is usually estimated that any given local election is decided by less than ten per cent of the electorate – the floaters, if you like. *Those* are the people you have to influence.

Don't underestimate the size of your own, personal circle of relatives, friends, acquaintances, workmates, fellow club members, business contacts, local tradespeople, and the rest. This personal vote has swayed many an election. Indeed, 'he's well-known around the area' is one comment which is almost invariably made when ward committee members sit down to consider possible candidates.

Lastly, anything can happen. In the district council elections of 1982, Conservative candidates were having a difficult time of it. Margaret Thatcher's first government had doubled VAT, unemployment was soaring, interest rates were high. Even sitting councillors who would normally have been considered 'safe' were contemplating 'spending more time with their families'.

Then, in mid-campaign, the Falklands conflict flared. Overnight, quite literally, there was a profound change in attitudes. Canvassers reported unprecedented swings in the reception they were getting on doorsteps. Conservatives gained seats up and down the country, and the subsequent general election assumed the proportions of a relative landslide.

Don't be deterred from accepting nomination by thoughts of inevitable defeat. You're in with a fighting chance. You wouldn't have got this far otherwise.

● *If you have any doubts – go for it!*

3
Pros and Cons

If you have any doubts – *go for it*!

Those were the words of advice which concluded the last chapter. The decision whether or not to stand for election is often quite a hairline one, and as most people tend to underestimate their own abilities, your first reaction may well be to say 'No'. This might be a bad decision from the point of view of your community and, for that matter, of your local Council. You *do* have something to offer, or you would not be considering the idea at all.

Here is a summary of the major 'fors' and 'againsts' of being a local councillor. Run down them, and see which way the balance tips for you.

PROS

Your status in the community
There is no doubt that as a local councillor you will be regarded as 'someone'. You will find that your social circle expands, that people notice you, and that your advice is sought on almost anything. People listen when you talk.

The people you meet
Local councillors have an entrée to places and events which you had probably not even considered before. Politicians and peers, singers and sportsmen, princes and pop stars – if they're visiting your area, you'll probably meet them. You'll probably get to know a fair few dustmen, too.

Being at the centre of things
If anything important is happening in your area, you'll get to know about it. Furthermore, you'll know about it in detail, and can speak on the subject with considerable authority. You'll know that a major employer is likely to relocate into your town before almost anyone else does, that a new restaurant is to open in the high street, and so on.

Influencing events

You won't just *know* about things – you'll be able to *do* something about a great many of them. If you don't like the design of a new building, you'll be able to say so in the places where it does most good, before planning permission is granted. If the line of a new road looks as if it's environmentally unacceptable, you'll be able to help to get it diverted.

Just as important, you'll be able to initiate things. If you see a crying need for more sports pitches, children's play equipment, old people's accommodation, you'll be able to set the ball rolling.

Helping people

Helping with individual problems is one of the most important – and most satisfying – aspects of local council work. Some things are quite simple – like getting a hole in the road mended, or repairing a defunct street light, for example. Other problems – getting families rehoused, for instance – can take months. But at least you are helping.

It can be fun

There's a great deal of pleasure in council work. You'll find yourself going places and doing things which are great fun. Remember, all councillors are, to some extent, part of the civic scene.

It's surprising, too, how many laughs you can find actually in the council chamber. Debates can often be witty and entertaining, officers (and members) can make hilarious *faux pas*. Turning your own polished phrases can be a source of enjoyment too.

CONS

The whipping boy

Everything which goes wrong is your fault. If gangs of lager louts are beating up the neighbourhood it's 'Why don't you do something about it?' If a dustman spills rubbish outside a neighbour's house, it's almost as if you went out and did it personally.

It really doesn't matter if the problem falls within the remit of the Council or not – you'll be expected to solve it. And you're a readily available person to blow off steam at.

No life of your own

If you're meeting lots of people then they're meeting you, too. To some extent, your private life is damaged, and the more visible you are, the more true this is.

You can't sit down in front of the TV without the knowledge that the phone might interrupt you, and indeed, your opportunities for a quiet evening at home are considerably reduced.

Drop into a pub for a quiet drink and someone will wonder if you're an alcoholic. Be seen around with someone who isn't your partner and eyebrows may be raised.

It's called 'public service', and that's what it is – public.

Little time for anything else

It's all very well being at the centre of things, but that's a time-consuming position to find yourself in. Time spent at meetings – in the council chamber and out – the hours you spend reading reams of paperwork, sheer thinking time, all conspire to ensure that your other interests are inclined to go by the board.

Beating your head against a wall

Council work can be frustrating. You may be able to see, quite clearly, what ought to be done, but other councillors may not agree with you, or the budget might not run to it.

Your ideas about priorities may not be the same as those of other people. As a new and inexperienced councillor, you can often feel as if you are beating your head against a wall.

People you can't help

You can't win 'em all, no matter how hard you try. It can be heartbreaking to find a young family living in unsatisfactory circumstances, while knowing that there are many other people worse off than they are, and that their chances of being allocated council accommodation within a reasonable time are nil.

You can't always help, however much you would like to.

It can be a drag

You'll be expected to turn out for meetings in all winds and weathers, no matter how hard you have been working all day. 'Didn't really feel like it' is no excuse for non-attendance in anyone's book.

You'll have to read a great deal of highly boring legalistic and technical information, and what's more, you're supposed to understand it.

And you may find that you don't very much like some of the people you're dealing with.

4
Getting Nominated

So you've made the decision. You'd like to try for a place on your local council. You now have to persuade a majority of the people who turn out and vote on election day that you are the right person for the job, remembering that two or three, or even more, other hopefuls have exactly the same idea, and may well be vastly more experienced than you are.

The large majority of candidates have the help and support of an organisation in achieving this aim. Such hopefuls may well have been approached by such an organisation, or the initiative may have come from the candidate himself (or herself). In either case, they have had to convince the appropriate bodies within that organisation that they are the right people for the job, and very often that applies to sitting councillors as well as political virgins. All of which means that you'll probably have to go through a selection process.

THE LOCAL COMMITTEE

These processes vary in different parts of the country, between political parties and even between branches of the same party, but almost always they involve likely candidates being interviewed by two separate bodies – a selection committee set up within the ward concerned, and one representing the local party organisation. To clarify that a little, a town of, say, 100,000 inhabitants may have over a dozen separate wards, each of which will have a local ward committee. At the top of that tree is the town's own party association. Each ward will have a selection committee – which commonly consists of the whole ward committee – and the central organisation will have a similar body, members probably drawn from all the constituent ward organisations, and including officers of the association concerned, plus senior sitting councillors.

The procedure adopted varies from place to place. Sometimes a central selection committee will draw up a list of suitable candidates, and circulate it around the wards. In other places the preferred procedure is to allow the wards to find their own candidates, and then submit them to interview by the central body. Sitting councillors, standing for re-election may be excused from the central part of the process, even, in some cases, being automatically selected without comment, but as a new aspirant for the job, you'll probably have two selection interviews to negotiate, whichever order they happen to come in.

Of the two committees your own ward committee is probably the more important. If they decide they want you, then it's unlikely that the central body will reject you, unless they have very good reason for doing so. Therefore, you should do homework on the problems facing the ward, and have some idea how you would tackle them if elected. In fact, you could start now. Here's an example of the sort of thing you might consider telling the committee.

Problems	*What I'll do if elected*
Need for a bypass to alleviate traffic problems.	Seek membership of Planning Committee and push for it.
Vandalism on playing field.	Talk to police about improved surveillance of area.
Spate of thefts and hooliganism.	Take the lead in setting up Neighbourhood Watch Scheme.

Of course, problems wouldn't *be* problems if there were easy solutions, so don't fall into the trap of saying you can solve everything. Talk to experienced councillors about possible approaches, find out what has already been done, and present yourself as a concerned, intelligent person, who is willing to learn, and who has ideas.

If you don't actually live in the ward, then you won't know so much about local issues, so you're going to have to find out before attending a selection meeting. There's only one way to do this – by spending time in the area, and by talking to people who really do know. It doesn't matter if the people you consult are members of the committee. They'll probably be impressed by the fact that you're doing your homework. Patronise the local pubs, cafes, libraries, and listen to people talk. Shop in the local shops, watch the local teams play football. Do anything you can think of to familiarise yourself with the ward, its problems and its advantages.

Self appraisal

It's also worthwhile to subject yourself to a little self-appraisal exercise. Identify your strengths and maximise them, be honest about your weaknesses and seek to ameliorate them. Time to get pen and paper out again.

Strengths
I live in the Ward.

- I know the problems. I have local support. I would be easily available. My children attend local schools.

I'm well-known locally.

- I am an active member of the drama group/church/trades union branch. That gives me local support.

I have useful experience.

- I am an experienced manager. I have financial expertise. I am used to committee work. I've brought up a family.

Weaknesses
I don't live in the Ward.

- That doesn't mean I can't be available. I have many friends/family connections in the Ward. I know the ward well through work/leisure activities.

I'm not a prominent local character.

- It's time there were some new faces about. I will work hard to make myself well known, with the committee's help. I am now in a work/family situation where I have time to make myself known and popular.

I'm just an ordinary working man/housewife.

- I can put the ordinary person's point of view. Bringing up a family is jolly useful experience. I'm a Council tenant, I can bring a fresh eye to problems.

You see, weaknesses may not be weaknesses at all, approached in the right way. Going through this exercise may surprise you by revealing the strengths you have, and it will enable you to approach the committee armed with answers.

These are just examples, of course, and a little thought will expand the list for you. And don't forget, two heads beat one, any day of the week, and it's worth asking your partner or a family member – even a known supporter in the branch organisation – to go through the exercise with you.

THE CENTRAL COMMITTEE

The central selection committee has a slightly different viewpoint. Its members will expect you to have an awareness of the political issues of the day, but no one requires the encyclopaedic knowledge expected from a budding MP, for example. Foreign issues don't usually come into the picture much.

What they will expect is to find a loyal member of the party, who is prepared to support his council political group. Most selection committees have a prepared standard question to elicit that fact. It may go, 'If elected, will you support the group at all times? If you find you can't, will you resign your seat?'

The obvious response is an unqualified 'yes', and if you feel you can do that, go ahead. However, you may not want to portray yourself as a political hack, mere vote fodder. There may be items of party policy with which you don't agree. If that is the case, then consider the following answer, taken more-or-less verbatim from an actual selection committee meeting in a West Midlands town.

Example

'To start with, I happen to be a Tory/Socialist/Democrat, so I shall obviously agree with the group in the vast majority of cases. On the odd occasion when I don't, then my observation is that such contentious issues don't arise suddenly. There is always time to consult with colleagues and reach a mutually agreeable compromise. If that proves impossible, then there would always be the possibility of taking the coward's way out, and abstaining from the vote, or absenting myself from it. If I felt so strongly that I felt I really must vote against the group, then, regretfully, I would have to do that. And in that case, then I would certainly consider resignation very carefully. In any case, I would never spring such a course of action on my colleagues without warning. There would be plenty of time to see if we couldn't sort things out, and there is usually a way to do this, with goodwill on all sides. But honestly, I can't see things ever getting to such an extreme situation.'

The candidate in question was adopted, and became a very senior Councillor and Mayor of his city.

Of course, the central selection committee will also be interested in local issues, but they are probably those which affect the whole authority area, rather than just one Ward. You may be asked, 'How do you feel about pedestrianisation, privatisation of leisure services, standards of street cleaning?' for example. Again, you will need to know your way around these areas, which will probably be those which have had a good airing in the local press, so there shouldn't be too many surprises.

You may also be asked about election expenses – often 'are you prepared to pay your own?' Sometimes, the Ward makes a contribution to the candidate's expenses, either from funds, or by running a special event for the purpose. It's as well to know about this before attending a central selection meeting.

SELECTION BY OTHER ORGANISATIONS

So far, we have been considering ways in which nationally-based political parties tend to run their election procedures, but, from time to time, other organisations also resolve to put forward candidates for the local council.

Examples would be tenants' associations, residents' associations, and similar bodies. Unfortunately, and with all the respect in the world, they tend to be more parochial in their outlook, and may well not have tried-and-true procedures, or quite such sophisticated organisations. It's therefore impossible to generalise about this situation. However, the basics remain true. Do your homework, know your area, work on your strengths and weaknesses.

GOING IT ALONE

The short advice would be – don't, not if you seriously want to win. Frankly, it's almost impossible. Even in large areas with a tradition of independent councillors, you'll find that some are more independent than others.

Often, while not paid-up members of a political party (and they may well be), the 'official' party organisation will know that the candidate in question is sympathetic to their own views, and they simply stay out of his way. They're a dwindling band, anyway, and likely to dwindle further as the latest round of local government reorganisations work their purposes out.

That's not to say that the thing is completely unheard of. Some years ago, a local ratepayer in a West Country city wrote a letter to the local press, complaining about the actions of the Mayor of the day. His Worship, perhaps inadvisably, wrote back, commenting that if Mr Bloggs didn't like the way he did things, then the remedy was for him to stand against him at the next election.

The complainant did. And won. And later became Mayor himself. There have to be special situations, however, for this to be a realistic proposition.

But perhaps you simply want to make a point, rather than having any real ambition to serve as a councillor. That's a perfectly reasonable and honourable course of action to take, as long as you know what you are doing, and why you are doing it.

The point is that, nowadays, you need an organisation behind you if you're going to be successful. The rugged individualist can't expect to stand on every doorstep in his ward, distribute literature through every letterbox, find enough poster sites to make an impact, and generally make a big enough noise to have a chance of winning. It's also an expensive luxury, because you don't get the economies of scale which are available to a party-backed candidate.

Still, Screaming Lord Sutch seems to enjoy it.

MAKING IT OFFICIAL

Having received the sponsorship of your chosen organisation, you now have to make your nomination official. There's nothing very difficult about this, but you do have time constraints, and you do have to be meticulous. If you have an Agent working for you, then some of the work will be taken off your shoulders, but there is an inescapable minimum which you have to do yourself.

The official most concerned in this process is the local **electoral registration officer**, who is an employee of the council. Don't confuse him with the **electoral returning officer**, who oversees the conduct of the whole election, and is usually the Chief Executive of the council, or perhaps the official solicitor or other senior officer of the council. (This differs slightly from the procedure at a general election, where the nominal returning officer is the Mayor or Chairman of the authority. Obviously, an elected member can't conduct an election to his own council.)

Electoral registration officers are normally friendly people who help all they can, but they do have to be very sure that everything is absolutely *right*, because any irregularity could make an election invalid.

Basically, there are two things you need from the electoral registration officer:

ELECTION OF COUNCILLOR(S)

for the

....**Ward of the**

....

Day of Election ....

CANDIDATE'S CONSENT TO NOMINATION

(to be given on or within one month before the last day for the delivery of nomination papers, and delivered at the place and within the time appointed for delivery of nomination papers)

I, (*name in full*)..

of (*home address in full*)..

.... hereby consent to my nomination as a candidate for

election as councillor for the ....ward of

the ....

I declare that on the day of my nomination I am qualified and that, if there is a poll on the day of election, I will be qualified to be so elected by virtue of being on that day or those days a Commonwealth citizen or citizen of the Republic of Ireland, who has attained the age of 21 years and that

(a)   I am registered as a local government elector for the area of the *[district] [London borough] named above in respect of (*qualifying address in full*)

     ....

     and my electoral number (*see Note below*) is..; or

(*b*)   I have during the whole of the twelve months preceding that day or those days occupied as owner or tenant the following land or other premises in that area (*description and address of land or premises*)..

     ....

     ....; or

(c)   My principal or only place of work during those twelve months has been in that area at (*give address of place of work and, where appropriate, name of employer*)..

     ....; or

(d)   I have during the whole of those twelve months resided in that area at (*give address in full*)...

     ....

I declare that to the best of my knowledge and belief I am not disqualified for being elected by reason of any disqualification set out in section 80 of the Local Government Act 1972, a copy of which is printed overleaf, and I do not hold a politically restricted post, within the meaning of Part I of the Local Government and Housing Act 1989, under a local authority within the meaning of that Part.

                         Signed ....

                         Date ....

Signed in my presence

Signature of witness ....

Name and address of witness(CAPITAL LETTERS) ....

....

* Delete whichever is inappropriate

NOTE.— A person's electoral number is his number in the register to be used at the election (including the distinctive letter of the parliamentary polling district in which he is registered) except that before publication of the register his number (if any) in the electors lists for that register shall be used instead.

        Cat. No. L.F. 4A.   SHAW & SONS Ltd., Shaway House, London, SE26 5AE   XLD 11837

                                                          [P.T.O.

Figure 2. A Consent to Nomination Form (continued overleaf).

Extracts from the **LOCAL GOVERNMENT ACT 1972 — Part V (as amended)**

Disqualifications for election and holding office as member of local authority.

Section 80.—(1) Subject to the provisions of section 81 below, a person shall be disqualified for being elected or being a member of a local authority if he—

(a) holds any paid office or employment (other than the office of chairman, vice-chairman or deputy chairman) appointments to which are or may be made or confirmed by the local authority or any committee or sub-committee of the authority or by a joint committee on which the authority are represented or by any person holding any such office or employment; or

(aa) holds any employment in a company which, in accordance with Part V of the Local Government and Housing Act 1989 other than section 73, is under the control of the local authority; or

(b) is a person who has been adjudged bankrupt, or made a composition or arrangement with his creditors; or

(d) has within five years before the day of election or since his election been convicted in the United Kingdom, the Channel Islands or the Isle of Man of any offence and has had passed on him a sentence of imprisonment (whether suspended or not) for a period of not less than three months without the option of a fine; or

(e) is disqualified for being elected or for being a member of that authority under Part III of the Representation of the People Act 1983 or under Part III of the Local Government Finance Act 1982.

(2) Subject to the provisions of section 81 below, a paid officer of a local authority who is employed under the direction of—

(a) a committee or sub-committee of the authority any member of which is appointed on the nomination of some other local authority; or

(b) a joint board, joint authority or joint committee on which the authority are represented and any member of which is so appointed;

shall be disqualified for being elected or being a member of that other local authority.

(3) Teachers in a school maintained but not established by a local education authority shall be in the same position as respects disqualification for office as members of the authority as teachers in a school established by the authority.

(5) For the purposes of subsection (1)(d) above, the ordinary date on which the period allowed for making an appeal or application with respect to the conviction expires or, if such an appeal or application is made, the date on which the appeal or application is finally disposed of or abandoned or fails by reason of the non-prosecution thereof shall be deemed to be the date of the conviction.

(6) In this section "local authority" includes a joint board and the Inner London Education Authority.

Exceptions to provisions of section 80.

Section 81.—(1) Where a person is disqualified under section 80 above by reason of having been adjudged bankrupt, the disqualification shall cease—

(a) unless the bankruptcy order made against that person is previously annulled, on his discharge from bankruptcy; and

(b) if the bankruptcy order is so annulled, on the date of annulment.

(2) Where a person is disqualified under section 80 above by reason of his having made a composition or arrangement with his creditors and he pays his debts in full, the disqualification shall cease on the date on which the payment is completed and in any other case it shall cease on the expiration of five years from the date on which the terms of the deed of composition or arrangement are fulfilled.

(4) Section 80(2) and (3) above shall not operate so as to disqualify any person by reason of his being a teacher, or otherwise employed, in a school, college or other educational institution maintained or assisted by a county council for being a member of a district council by reason that the district council nominates members of the education committee of the county council.

Figure 2 (continued). A Consent to Nomination Form.

● A Consent to Nomination Form

You have to agree to be nominated. This is done by signing and returning a consent to nomination form on or within one month of the last day for the delivery of nomination papers, and it must be delivered to the place appointed for delivery of nomination papers. This form also states that the candidate is qualified to stand for election on both nomination day, and on the day of the election. The form also needs witnessing.

● Nomination Papers

In effect, ten people who are qualified to vote for you must signify, in the approved manner, that they agree your nomination. This does not necessarily commit them to voting for you. The ten voters consist of a **proposer**, a **seconder**, and eight **assenters**. The completed paper therefore bears ten names, plus signatures, and also the electoral number – as indicated on the appropriate electoral roll – of everyone concerned. A nomination paper also carries your own full name (surname first) and home address, and can, if you wish, also include a description of not more than six words. Such a description may refer to your political affiliation – or lack of it – but needn't include your rank, profession or calling. Taken together with the other particulars, there must be sufficient evidence to identify you unequivocally.

The returning officer is required to publish a statement of persons nominated, not later than noon on the seventeenth day before the election, which means that, normally, your nomination papers have to be handed in no later than noon on the nineteenth day before the election. The timescale usually means that you don't have more than a few days to get nomination forms signed and handed to the electoral registration officer.

Indeed, things can be quite tight. In many cases, one agent acts for all the candidates of a political party – perhaps a dozen or so. That probably involves him in handing all nomination papers in at once, and he needs a couple of days to go over each one with a fine tooth-comb to eliminate errors, and, if necessary, to get a candidate to get another form signed.

Getting your papers signed

Note 'papers', plural, not 'paper', singular. It's very easy to make a small error when getting your signatures, and a little bit of 'belt and braces' goes a long way to make things safe for you. Many a

Nomination Paper

ELECTION OF COUNCILLOR(S)

for the

.... **Ward of the**

....

Day of Election ....

We, the undersigned, being local government electors for the said ward do hereby nominate the under-mentioned person as a candidate at the said election.

NO. OF NOMINATION PAPER IN ORDER OF DELIVERY ...		
DATE DELIVERED	HOUR DELIVERED	INITIALS

Candidate's Surname	Other Names in full	Description (if any)	Home address in full

	ELECTORAL NUMBER (See Note 3)	
SIGNATURES	Distinctive Letter(s)	Number

Proposer ....

Seconder ....

Figure 3. A Nomination Paper.

We, the undersigned, being local government electors for the said ward, do hereby assent to the foregoing nomination.

1. ....

2. ....

3. ....

4. ....

5. ....

6. ....

7. ....

8. ....

NOTE

1. The attention of candidates and electors is drawn to the rules for filling up nomination papers and other provisions relating to nomination contained in elections rules in Schedule 2 to the Local Elections (Principal Areas) Rules 1986.

2. Where a candidate is commonly known by some title he may be described by his title as if it were his surname.

3. A person's electoral number is his number in the register to be used at the election (including the distinctive letter of the parliamentary polling district in which he is registered) except that before publication of the register his number (if any) in the electors lists for that register shall be used instead.

4. An elector may not—

(*a*) subscribe more nomination papers than there are vacancies to be filled in the electoral area in which the election is held; or

(*b*) subscribe a nomination paper for more than one electoral area in the same district or London borough.

5. A person whose name is entered in the register or electors lists may not subscribe a nomination paper if the entry gives as the date on which he will become of voting age a date later than the day fixed for the poll.

Cat. No. L.E. 4. Printed by SHAW & SONS Ltd, Shaway House, London, SE26 5AE   XLZ 4607 would-be candidate has lost the chance to stand because of a mistake on the paper, and lack of time to get a new one signed and delivered. And the two papers have to be different, because no elector is allowed to sign more papers than there are vacancies to be filled. Assuming that only one seat is to be contested in your Ward, therefore, you can't get any supporter to sign both of your nomination papers.

Even where a whole District Council is to be elected, and therefore there are three vacancies to be filled in your ward, you may well find that your two colleagues want to approach the same people for their signatures, and they won't thank you for pinching two available signatures. In effect, therefore, you're not looking for ten people to sign for you, but twenty, which can be a sizeable chore.

Of course, there is nothing to stop you asking two or more members of the same family to sign your paper, as long as they all appear on the electoral roll, but do remember, that the names of the nominators on one of your papers are going to be published on the **notice of poll** which is posted up outside each polling station, and undue repetition of the same name doesn't exactly give electors the impression that you have widespread support. If you do approach, say, husband and wife, then it's as well to get them to sign separate papers.

Signatures must enable the nominator to be unmistakably identified as the elector whose number also appears on the paper. It could well be, therefore, that the normal signature isn't good enough for the electoral registration officer. For example, if an elector appears on the roll as 'Tom. D. Harry', but normally uses his middle name and signs himself, 'Dick Harry', then the registration officer might take the view that this may not be the same person as the one appearing in the roll alongside the number quoted. The safe thing to do is ask your nominators to sign precisely as their names appear in the electoral roll, regardless of how they normally sign.

The **electoral number** must appear alongside each name, just as it does in the electoral roll, but in addition, what is known as the **distinctive letters** must appear too. These aren't printed alongside every name in the roll, because they normally refer to the whole ward in question. You'll find them printed on the front cover of the electoral roll, a copy of which you are entitled to, and which will probably have been supplied to you by your agent.

Who you approach to sign, within your ward, is up to you. Your ward committee members obviously offer a good place to start, but you'll have to be sure that they all appear on the roll. If you live in the ward yourself, you probably won't have any difficulty about finding twenty names. If you don't then your committee will be able to point you in the right direction. Obviously, in that case, your own family probably won't be able to support you in this way.

The easy thing to do is to find your names from known activists, but it's worth remembering that there is an opportunity here to approach 'non-politicals' who are well known in other fields, and therefore claim their support. It isn't a bad thing, for example, to have the signature of the Chairperson of the local Community Association on your paper, and therefore, hopefully, on the notice of poll. 'Ah! Old so-and-so is supporting him. Must be a good choice!' is the reaction you are seeking.

5
Before Your Campaign

Now we must backtrack a little. There is a lot to be done before your campaign starts, some of it before nomination day. Let's start by outlining the official timetable of events.

TIMETABLE OF EVENTS

Normally, local elections take place on the first Thursday in May, although the Secretary of State for the Environment does have it in his power to vary that if he wishes. By-elections are a different matter. If a seat becomes vacant for any reason, then a by-election may be held at any time, *except* within six months of the date when the seat would have fallen vacant anyway. The election period lasts for something over four weeks, the first event being the notice of election which appears outside every polling station in the area concerned.

Things are complicated, however, by phenomena known as *dies non*. Ignoring the Latin, this means that Saturdays, Sundays, Maundy Thursday, Good Friday and Bank holidays don't count and are disregarded for the purposes of calculating the timetable. In the case of a by-election, Christmas Eve and Christmas Day are added to that list, but no one in their right mind would call an election over the Christmas period if it could possibly be avoided. Here's the schedule of events.

Event	*Latest day and time*
Notice of election	25th day before election day.
Delivery of nomination papers to registration officer	Noon on 19th day before election day.
Publication of statement of names of people nominated	Noon on 17th day before election day.
Notice of withdrawal	Noon on 16th day before election day.

Notice of appointment of election agent	Noon on 16th day before election day.
Notice of poll	6th day before election day.
Notice of appointment of polling or counting agents	5th day before election day.

A little explanation may be required on one or two matters.

Notice of election and notice of poll

As already mentioned, a **notice of election** is posted at every polling station at least 25 days before the election takes place. This simply states that a seat or seats are to fall vacant, and that if they are contested, then an election will take place on such-and-such a date. It also tells you from where nomination papers can be obtained, and the last day on which they must be completed and delivered. Around a week before the election, the notice of election is replaced by a **notice of poll**, which tells you who has been nominated for the ward. It also lists the polling stations in that ward, and which residents of which streets vote at each polling station in the ward. This is also the notice which carries the names of all the people who signed one of your nomination papers.

Deadline for withdrawal

After noon on the sixteenth day before the election – you can't. Even if you change your mind, flee the country or walk under a bus, then after that day, the election goes ahead as if nothing had happened, with your name proudly on the notice of poll. Note, too, that if you withdraw after nomination day, then you can't be replaced, and your organisation goes unrepresented.

Polling and counting agents

Happily, polling agents are an anachronism in this country. The idea is that you can appoint one person to attend each polling station to detect the offence known as **personation** – the practice of pretending to be someone else so as to steal their vote. Nowadays, in Great Britain, appointment of polling agents is just about unheard of. Counting agents, attending the count to represent your interests, are a different matter, and we'll get around to those a little later.

ABSENT VOTERS

People who are qualified to vote, but, for one reason or another, can't attend a polling station on the day, can use their franchise, as long as their reason for absence isn't completely frivolous. There are arrangements for service personnel, for example, and proxy votes can be obtained for a variety of other reasons. But the one which will concern your campaign most is the postal vote.

Postal votes

Postal votes come in two categories. Someone who is an invalid, housebound, or confined to bed permanently, in hospital or elsewhere, can obtain a once-and-for-all postal vote. All that is necessary is for a doctor to testify to that effect on the appropriate form. Postal ballot papers will be sent to the elector at every election, including general and European elections, from then on.

But many postal votes belong to the other category – the one which applies to one election only. If a voter, appearing on the electoral roll, knows that attendance on polling day will be impossible, then application can be made to the returning officer, enabling the vote to be cast by post.

In recent years, conditions required for such voting have been relaxed considerably. Nowadays, if someone is going to be away on holiday, absent on business, or on a training course, for example, then the application will be granted.

The snag about this is the time scale. Ignoring *dies non*, applications for postal votes have to be returned by noon on the thirteenth day before the election – around a week after nomination day, and therefore just as the campaign is getting under way. This, in practice, means that you won't pick up many postal votes while canvassing, and it's worth your while to make an effort to find once-only absent voters, by whatever method you can, before the campaign starts. A mention in a pre-election newsletter is one thing you can provide, for example.

If you have old people's homes or nursing homes in your ward, then a chat with the warden, or whoever is in charge, can pay big dividends. Such people don't want their residents to lose their votes, and you'll usually find them very co-operative. They will usually take supplies of postal vote application forms, and encourage people to use them. Of course, you may be supplying votes for the opposition by this method, but they will be doing the same for you, and things average out. Many a local election has been won and lost by a margin much smaller than the number of postal votes received, so you really should put some effort into it.

One recent innovation concerns people who fall ill after the

DISTRICT OF GLOUCESTER

NOTICE OF ELECTION

ELECTION OF DISTRICT COUNCILLORS AND PARISH COUNCILLORS FOR THE ELECTORAL AREAS AS SPECIFIED BELOW

NOTICE IS HEREBY GIVEN THAT—

1. Elections are to be held of District Councillors and Parish Councillors for the undermentioned Electoral Areas. The numbers of Councillors to be elected are as shown in Columns No. 2 (District) and No. 4 (Parish) in the Table hereunder:

FOR **DISTRICT** COUNCIL ELECTIONS		FOR **PARISH** COUNCIL ELECTIONS	
1 Name of District Ward	2 Number of District Councillors to be elected	3 Name of Parish and Parish Wards	4 Number of Parish Councillors to be elected
BARNWOOD	1	QUEDGELEY	
BARTON	1		
EASTGATE	1	QUEDGELEY CENTRAL	4
HUCCLECOTE	1	QUEDGELEY EAST	2
KINGSHOLM	1	QUEDGELEY FIELDCOURT	3
LINDEN	1	QUEDGELEY SEVERN VALE	3
LONGLEVENS	1	QUEDGELEY SOUTH	4
MATSON	1		
PODSMEAD	1		
QUEDGELEY	2		
TUFFLEY	1		
WESTGATE	1		

2. Nomination Papers must be delivered at my office at the North Warehouse, The Docks, Gloucester on any day after the date of this notice, but not later than noon on Friday, the 5th day of April, 1991.

3. Forms of nomination paper may be obtained from the undersigned, who will at the request of any elector for the said Wards prepare a nomination paper for signature.

4. If any election is contested, the Poll will take place on Thursday, 2nd May, 1991.

5. Electors and their proxies should take note that applications to be treated as absent voters and other applications and notices about postal or proxy voting must reach the Electoral Registration Officer at the North Warehouse, The Docks, Gloucester not later than **NOON ON MONDAY, THE 15th DAY OF APRIL NEXT** (or where applications are made after the closing date in accordance with the Representation of the People Regulations in the event of unforeseen circumstances which relate to the applicant's health) by NOON on Wednesday, 24th April if they are to be effective for these Elections.

R. A. COOK
Returning Officer

DATED this 19th day of March, 1991.
NORTH WAREHOUSE, THE DOCKS, GLOUCESTER.

Printed by John Jennings (Printers) Ltd., Unit 12, Madleaze Industrial Estate, Bristol Road, Gloucester
Published by R. A. Cook, Returning Officer, North Warehouse, The Docks, Gloucester

Figure 4. A typical Notice of Election.

DISTRICT OF GLOUCESTER

NOTICE OF POLL

I hereby give notice that a Poll for the Election of One Councillor for the

BARTON WARD

of the said District, will be taken on

THURSDAY, THE 7th DAY OF MAY, 1987

and will commence at eight o'clock in the morning and be kept open till nine o'clock in the afternoon of the same day and no longer.

Also that the several Candidates remaining validly nominated, and the names of the proposer seconder and assenters who signed the nomination paper of each Candidate, are as follows:—

NAMES OF CANDIDATES		HOME ADDRESS IN FULL	DESCRIPTION	NAMES OF PROPOSER
SURNAME	OTHER NAMES IN FULL		(if any)	SECONDER AND ASSENTERS
COSSTICK	David Goodwin	6 Faraday Close, Tredworth, Gloucester	The Labour Party Candidate	**Proposer:** Mark E. Kills **Seconder:** Susan J. Killy **Assenters:** Michael Speke, Evan J. Garwood, Jennifer Garwood, Philip C. Downs, Dudley S. Davis, Dorel P. Davis, Rose Workman, Anthony E. Workman.
STEVENSON	Colin William	94 High Street, Tredworth, Gloucester	The Conservative Party Candidate	**Proposer:** Andrew Gravells **Seconder:** Florence B. Pollard **Assenters:** Toma Moss, Marjorie E. V. Grigg, Frederick M. Grigg, Irene M. Langdon, Suleman I. Kholwadia, Ayesha S. Kholwadia, Leonard G. Proctor, Olive Tartaglia.
YOUNG	Lilian Ivy	33 Warwick Avenue, Gloucester	Liberal SDP Alliance	**Proposer:** Stanley F. Skinner **Seconder:** Alison I. Easton **Assenters:** Coral Presley, Mary Smith, John F. King, Yolanda Russo, Sarah R. Hill, Patrick A. Hill, Thomas H. L. Olliffe, Eileen G. Hughes

Also that the description of the polling district, and the situation of each polling station, and the description of persons entitled to vote thereat, are as follow:—

DESCRIPTION OF POLLING DISTRICT	SITUATION OF POLLING STATION	DESCRIPTION OF PERSONS ENTITLED TO VOTE AT EACH POLLING STATION
BARTON WARD **Polling District A**	**TREDWORTH JUNIOR SCHOOL** High Street Entrance	**Electors Registered for:—** Belgrove Terrace, Brook Street, Carmarthen Street, Conduit Street 1-35 and 38-2, Dainty Street, Daventry Terrace, Dynevor Street, Falkner Street, Farm Mews 2, 3 & 5, Goodyere Street — even numbers, Grove Street, High Street 94-2, Howard Street — odd numbers, Llandilo Street, Midland Road 13-52, Morpeth Street, Regent Street, Ryecroft Street, even numbers, Conduit Street 37-79 and 90-40, Dorrit Close, Faraday Close, Furlong Road, Hanman Road.
		High Street 158-98, Howard Street, even numbers, Huxley Road, Knowles Road, Nelson Street, Osric Road, Slaney Street, St. Aldwyn Road, Tredworth Road 1-61 and 126-2 Wellesley Street, Wheatstone Road, Bathurst Road, Clevedon Road, Hartland Road, Highworth Road, Parry Road, Tredworth Road 170-128.
	HATHERLEY INFANTS SCHOOL Hatherley Road	Adelaide Street, Albany Street, Barton Street 386-350, Dora Walk, Ducie Street, Hatherley Road, High Street — odd numbers, Leonard Road, Maldon Gardens, Massey Parade, Massey Road, Matson Place, Melbourne Street East, Melbourne Street West, Moor Street, Moreton Street, Percy Street, Sybil Road, Tarrington Road, The Laurels, Tredworth Road 65-183, Upton Street — even numbers and The Conifers, Vicarage Road, Victory Road.
	FINLAY JUNIOR SCHOOL Tredworth Road	Avening Road, Bibury Road, Dickens Close 4-21, Finlay Road 100-2, Northfield Road 1-103 and 112-2, Sapperton Road, Selwyn Road 1-19.

North Warehouse, The Docks, Gloucester   Dated this 23rd day of April, 1987

Printed by John Jennings (Gloucester) Ltd, Brunswick Road, Gloucester
Published by H. R. T. Shackleton, Returning Officer, North Warehouse, The Docks, Gloucester.

H. R. T. SHACKLETON
Returning Officer

Figure 5. A Notice of Poll.

official date for acceptance of postal votes. If an elector breaks a leg, or goes into early labour, for example, after the thirteenth day before the election, then application may be made for a postal vote until noon on the sixth day before election day. Again, the form must be witnessed by a doctor.

You, or your representative, may attend both the issuing of postal votes, and the counting of them on election day. You need not give notice of appointment of the people to attend until the last moment, and depending on the facilities available, you may well be able to send more than one person along. The issue of postal votes won't tell you very much, but the count, which usually takes place during the afternoon of election day, may give you an early indication of how things are going.

YOUR ELECTION AGENT

There is enough to be said about the duties and responsibilities of an election agent to fill a book the size of this one. Indeed, it's a profession in its own right. Briefly, your agent is the person who oversees the conduct of your campaign, makes sure that the law isn't infringed, looks after the expenses, often sees to the production of literature, and generally keeps you on the straight and narrow. The major piece of advice would be to do exactly what your agent tells you, no more and no less.

For example, you may be asked to take part in a local radio programme on the election, and could be pardoned for grabbing the chance with both hands. But your agent would probably say, 'Hold on a minute. Who else is appearing?' The point is that you aren't allowed, under the law, to do any such thing unless you have the permission of all the other candidates in your ward to do so. In practice, that often means that all the relevant candidates take part in the broadcast. Otherwise, they'd be mad to give you the chance for extra publicity. This is just one example of the pitfalls which await the unwary, and which a good agent is there to circumvent.

Appointing an agent
Electoral regulations oblige you to appoint an agent, and you must give notice of that appointment to the returning officer by noon on the sixteenth day before the election. If you don't do so, you are assumed to have appointed yourself. The agent so appointed must also supply a written declaration of acceptance of the office.

Generally speaking, where political parties are concerned, one agent is appointed centrally, and runs things for all of the wards in

BOROUGH CONSTITUENCY OF GLOUCESTER

DISTRICT OF GLOUCESTER

Parliamentary Electors	Polling District . . . . . . K (Hucclecote Ward)
Local Government Electors }	County Electoral Division . . HUCCLECOTE
	District of Gloucester . . . . HUCCLECOTE WARD
European Assembly Electors . . . . . . COTSWOLD CONSTITUENCY	

REGISTER OF ELECTORS

(Qualifying date, 10th October 1987)

IN FORCE 16th FEBRUARY 1988 to 15th FEBRUARY 1989

NOTE — The number printed immediately before an Elector's name means that the elector reaches voting age on, and will be able to vote at Elections held on or after that day during the currency of the Register.
L printed before a name indicates that the elector is not entitled to vote in respect of that entry at Parliamentary Elections.
F printed before a name indicates that the elector is entitled to vote in respect of that entry at Parliamentary and European Assembly Elections only.
E printed before a name indicates that the elector is entitled to vote in respect of that entry at European Assembly Elections only.

H. R. T. SHACKLETON
North Warehouse, The Docks, Gloucester *15th February 1988*   *Electoral Registration Office*

POLLING DISTRICT No. 5011

BOROUGH CONSTITUENCY OF GLOUCESTER - POLLING DISTRICT (K) - HUCCLECOTE WARD

No.	Name and Address		No.	Name and Address		No.	Name and Address	
	001-BARNACRE DRIVE			**001-BARNACRE DRIVE**(cont.)			**002-BURLEIGH CROF**	
1	Rolfe, Lorraine M.	1	35	Headland, Philip C.	32	68	Pockett, Florence M.	
2	Rolfe, Peter W.	1	36	Headland, Roger K.	32	69	Pockett, Frank R.	
3	Fluck, Beryl A.	3	37	Twycross, Giulia.	30	70	Knight, David.	
4	Fluck, Robert A.	3	38	Twycross, Gordon C.	30	71	Knight, John E.	
5	Wyman, Phylis E D.	3	39	Thompson, Alexander.	28	72	Knight, Molly E.	
6	Young, Andrew R.	5	40	Thompson, Rosemary J.	28	73	Chavda, Bhikhulal G.	
7	Young, Jean M.	5	41	Gidman, Joan.	26	74	Chavda, Harvidya B.	
8	Young, Nicola J.	5	42	Gidman, Stanley H.	26	75	Lawn, Derrick.	
9	Young, Robert M.	5	43	Benbow, Diana M.	24	76	Lawn, Marilyn A.	
10	Jones, Gwynfryn L.	7	44	Benbow, Michael J.	24	77	Gough, Maureen A.	
11	Jones, Maud.	7	45	Benbow, Rosalind M.	24	78	Gough, Richard J F.	
12	Hoepfner, Margaret A.	9	46	Plowman, Julie A.	22	79	Jones, Jacqueline E.	
13	Wright, Alison A.	11	47	Plowman, Keith.	22	80	Jones, Leslie G.	
14	Barnes, Frances M.	13	48	Moore, Christopher J.	18	81	Foad, Andrew P.	
15	Barnes, Gary R.	13	49	Moore, Gerrie T.	18	82	Foad, Josephine A.	
16	Barnes, Karin L.	13	50	Childs, Glyn B.	16	83	Foad, Peter S.	
17	Barnes, Nigel P.	13	51	Childs, Janet.	16	84	Cook, Andrew.	
18	Hughes, Grace.	15	52	Lewis, Bernice D.	14	85	Cook, Angela.	
19	Elkins, Craig.	17	53	Haman, Peter H P.	12	86	Cook, Colin.	
20	Elkins, Gerald B.	17	54	Haman, Vera D.	12	87	Cook, Marion A.	
21	Elkins, Patricia A.	17	55	Beazer, John W.	10	88	Cooling, Grace E.	
22	Elkins, Steven.	17	56	Beazer, Margaret.	10	89	West, Alfred M.	1
23	Wetson, Patrick R.	19	57	Beazer, Stephen J.	10	90	West, Nellie A.	1
24	Wetson, Susan M.	19	58	Dunne, Adrian F.	8	91	Hawkins, Herbert K.	1
25	Clutterbuck, Richard D.	40	59	Dunne, John J.	8	92	Card, Annie.	1
26	Clutterbuck, Shirley P.	40	60	Sutlow, Colin P.	6	93	Card, Emma J.	1
27	Clutterbuck, Stephen D.	40	61	Sutlow, Kathleen.	6	94	Card, William.	1
28	Wilkins, Carole E.	38	62	Lancaster, Janet.	4	95	Perry, Michael.	1
29	Joyner, Ivy M.	36	63	Lancaster, Paul.	4	96	Perry, Patricia R.	1
30	Joyner, Josephine.	36	64	Crandon, Anita S.	2	97	Shute, Antony P.	1
31	Holmes, Norma B.	34	65	Crandon, Ian A.	2	98	Shute, Christopher A.	1
32	Holmes, Peter.	34	66	Crandon, Shirley S.	2	99	Shute, Heather.	1
33	Headland, Brian G.	32	67	Crandon, Trevor A	2	100	Shute, Malcolm P.	1
34	Headland, Jennifer.	32				101	Shute, Peter W.	1

Printed by Systemset, Stotfold, Hitchin, Herts, for the Electoral Registration Officer of the Borough Constituency of Gloucester

Figure 6. Extract from a typical Electoral Roll.

that area, which gives an overall view of everything that is happening, and yields economies of scale in the production of literature, for example. The system also gives the electoral registration officer one central point to which he can refer in case of complaint, or any other matter called to his attention. There are other advantages too, which will emerge as we proceed.

YOUR CAMPAIGN MANAGER

If your agent is the strategist, then your campaign manager is the tactician. He or she is your own personal guide, mentor and friend, with only your ward to worry about. Their job is to attend to the minutiae of the election in your ward – arranging canvassers and tellers, getting literature delivered, making sure typing is done, finding and arranging committee rooms on the day, and all the rest. It's perfectly possible to act as your own campaign manager, but it's something to be avoided. You have quite enough to worry about getting yourself seen, known and elected, without having to worry about the staff work.

Your campaign manager, by whatever title he or she is known, will probably be appointed by your ward committee, although your own wishes in the matter will certainly be consulted. Ideally, he should have an encyclopaedic knowledge of the ward with a very wide range of contacts. Experience is very valuable too, and above all, a flair for administration is required.

You're going to be seeing your campaign manager every day for weeks. If the pair of you don't get on very well, then you have a recipe for disaster, right there. You'll have your own ideas about how your campaign should be run, and your manager will try to fulfill them, although his superior experience and knowledge may lead him to modify or change them completely. Again – do what you're told, when you're told to do it. The campaign manager's job is to package and sell you just like any other product.

THE ELECTORAL ROLL

The electoral roll for your ward is your bible. You can't really do much without it. As a candidate, you will have your own copy, but your ward organisation will need at least two more – one for your campaign manager, and one which is there to be cut up into small pieces! That one is dissected into streets and stuck down on cards, for the use of canvassers.

Just about the first thing to do in your campaign is to sit down with your electoral roll and go through it street by street, ticking off families which you know, or which you feel you should call upon personally for other reasons. Apart from anything else, the exercise will make you familiar with the roll, the order the streets appear in, where there are blocks of flats, houses in multiple occupation and similar premises which may need special attention. You won't, for example, want to send a canvasser who isn't quite as agile as he used to be climbing several staircases in an old house converted into flats.

The electoral roll will also show you where service voters live, and by placing a date alongside the appropriate names, where there are electors voting for the first time because they have attained the age of eighteen within the currency of the roll. Read intelligently, the electoral roll can yield a surprising amount of information, and you can't have too much of that.

YOUR LITERATURE

This is no time to be modest. As already mentioned, for a few weeks, you are just as much a product as anything you see advertised in the media. You must, in fact, be sold. Unfortunately, most of the methods of promotion open to you can be classified as 'junk mail', so you have to find ways to make sure that your literature is actually read. You can't do this by simply throwing money at the problem, because of the limits placed on election expenses, but there are other ways of getting your message across.

Your photograph

One common denominator running through most of your literature is your photograph. You want people to recognise you when they see you so you should take every opportunity to enable them to do so. It may be that the extra costs involved preclude you from featuring a photograph absolutely everywhere – a large picture on a poster is prohibitively expensive, for example – but any piece of literature which can bear a picture should do so.

It's worth thinking about the elements of a good election photograph, and the first one has already been mentioned; it's there to help you to be recognised. Pictures of you playing with the kids or taking the dog for a walk may present you as an attractive human being, but also mean that your facial features are reproduced as a very small area of the picture. Add to that the vagaries of printing and graphic reproduction, and the 'recognition factor' rapidly reduces to infinity. So, for practical purposes, you are confined to head-and-shoulders, or at the most, three-quarters portraits.

Obviously, you're going to look neat and tidy, have your hair done, and generally appear as presentable as possible. But here, one of the first rules of candidacy, or for that matter, of membership of a local authority, must be brought to bear. Engrave it on your heart.

Don't try to be anything that you're not.

Too many people 'knew you when', and you can't keep it up, anyway. Much better to show yourself in your true colours, warts and all, if you like – just as long as the warts are attractive.

In the context of your election photograph, this has one or two implications. If you are a lady who is usually seen with your hair tied back in a French roll, then don't be photographed with your hair down, as if you were going to a ball in a long dress. If you usually wear a tee shirt and jeans, don't be tempted to dress up in a business suit and tie (the converse is also true. Don't dress down-market in an attempt to appear trendy). If you are a member of your local rugby club, wear the club sweater or tie – other members will be voting.

The background against which your portrait is shot can be useful, too, and may persuade you not to have your picture taken in a studio. A keen gardener, for example, can say something about himself by being photographed in his garden. Perhaps you should consider seating yourself at a desk with a bookshelf in the background. A housewife might advertise the fact by utilising her kitchen. But beware: cluttered backgrounds detract from the subject, you – and look even worse when inexpensively reproduced on a printed page.

Anyone who has ever tried to take his own passport photo in one of those slot-machine booths will know that facial expression is very difficult. An earnest smile can easily emerge as a silly grin. It's best to allow your face to make its own mind up, and select the picture you like best from several shots.

Finally, taking this sort of picture is a professional job. Unless you know a very good amateur, it's worth investing a few pounds in employing someone to take yours.

Your election address

This is your major leaflet, and probably won't be distributed until fairly late in the campaign. However, it does take a fair amount of preparation and printing, so it will have been organised well before nomination day. It's frequently known as 'the glossy', even though more and more frequently, these days, it is printed on cartridge paper rather than the traditional glossy art paper. All sorts of formats are used for election addresses, but the vast majority have certain elements in common.

To start with, you'll probably only be asked to supply text for one side of the paper. The other will have been organised by the central committee, and will set out policies covering the whole area. The other side will refer directly to your own ward. You will probably be asked to supply three elements:

- your photograph

- a short biography

- a letter to your electorate

You'll have help preparing these elements, and will probably be advised as to the number of words you can write for each.

So what do you write in your 'bio'? The short answer is 'anything which will help you get elected'. If you were born in the town, that's important. People like to read about family details. Did you go to school locally? What do you do for a living? Above all, why should people vote for you rather than the opposition? To repeat: this is no time to be modest, and the fact that this section of the leaflet is written in the third person enables you to be more self-promoting than you can in your letter.

Remember the old salesman's ploy of 'features and benefits'. The fact that you are a mother of two isn't of particular interest. That's a feature. The benefit is that, being a mother of two gives you the ability to represent similar people from a position of first-hand knowledge and commitment. Try this:

'Jean has two small children, and therefore feels strongly about education and nursery facilities.'

If you're a manager you know about 'good housekeeping'. If you hold the chair of a local organisation, you are experienced in committee work. If you are a sportsman, you have strong feelings about leisure provision. Go through another pen-and-paper exercise. Think of the things you can claim, and what benefits they give you, and therefore the elector if he supports you.

A typical election 'bio'
Here's an example of an election bio. It's quite fictional, but will help you in preparing yours.

BILL FERGUSON

Bill is a native of Bilberry, is well acquainted with the problems of the area, and has very decided ideas about how they should be tackled. He is married, with a son at King Edward's School, and believes that it is vital to provide employment opportunities for school leavers in the area. He runs his own small business, which gives him an insight into getting value for money – especially public money.

He also coaches a local youth football team, and would like to see leisure facilities for young people extended, helping reduce the incidence of vandalism in our streets and parks, and keeping the standards of health and fitness high.

Bill is a forthright, no nonsense, man who will make sure that your interests on the Council are vigorously represented. He lives in High Street and is a familiar figure at the Community Centre, so will always be available to help with individual problems. By voting for him, you vote for local knowledge, commitment and very considerable ability.

You get the idea? Features and benefits all the way.

A typical 'Dear Elector' letter
The tone of your first-person letter is completely different. Here, you will obviously want to influence the voter, but you can't be quite so blatant about it. This is also a good spot to make a point about problems specific to your ward. But again, 'Don't try to be anything you're not'. The letter should read as if you, and no one else, has written it; turns of phrase should be those you would normally use in conversation. One good ploy is to sit down and imagine that the person to whom you are writing is sitting opposite you. Then write precisely the way you would if you were talking to him. And don't forget 'features and benefits'. Example:

Dear Elector,

I'm delighted to have been selected as a Candidate in the forth-coming District Council Election, and I promise you that, when elected, I will represent you to the very best of my ability.

There is much to be done in Bilberry, and while I don't pretend to be able to solve all our problems immediately, I will set about them as forcibly as I can. For example, it is high time that mothers taking children to Bilberry Road School had a pedestrian crossing across the main road, and one of my first actions will be to raise the matter in the appropriate places.

Being actively involved in sport myself, I also know how important it is that we have satisfactory changing accommodation on the playing field. More use of the facilities provided will help prevent the amount of vandalism which has occurred there.

In asking you for your support on May 3rd, I assure you that the interests of your neighbours and yourself will always come before narrow political considerations as far as I am concerned. I hope to meet you personally during the course of the campaign.

Sincerely,

Bill Ferguson

Let's analyse that letter a little:

Dear Elector	It doesn't have to be 'Elector'. It could be 'Resident' or even 'Neighbour', if you think that's appropriate.
I'm delighted	Of course you are. Not only is it an honour, but it gives you a chance to do something for your ward.
When elected	Show confidence. If you don't, then no one else will have confidence in you. Of course you're going to win! A vote for anyone else is wasted.
There is much to be done. . .	The opposition has fallen down on the job. Blatant 'knocking' of your opponent leaves a bad taste in the mouths of many people, but you can criticise by implication. A stiletto is more effective than a cutlass.
I don't pretend. . .	Never make promises you may not be able to keep. They'll come back to haunt you.

One of my first actions. . .	You have ideas, and know how to set about things.
In asking for your support	In salesman's language, 'Don't forget to ask for the order'.
I hope to meet you	You're working very hard.
Sincerely	The subscription and name can with advantage be reproduced as a facsimile, in your own handwriting. You can also, if you wish, add your own address and/ or phone number. If you don't actually live in the ward, however, there may not be much point in advertising the fact.

There are, of course, other important elements of an election address, such as date and times of poll. However, you won't normally have to worry about them because they will be handled centrally, and you have far too much to do to get involved in too much detail.

Introduction cards

Everyone has an election address, of course, and usually some form of introductory literature as well. One very effective and labour-saving way to produce this is in the form of an introduction card. This isn't universally used, so it may be that your central organisation won't be providing one, and that your ward organisation will have to produce it.

An introduction card is used while canvassing. It can be slipped easily through letterboxes, if no one's at home when your canvasser calls, and gives your team something to leave behind when they are talking on doorsteps. You therefore don't have to organise a separate distribution for it. Any excess can also be used to give to voters who are picked up by car on election day.

The format is simple. On one side there is simply your name, with an exhortation to vote for you, the date and times of the election. The other carries your photograph and some well-chosen words, which can be precisely the same as those you use as a 'bio' on your election address, but will preferably be written especially for the job.

Last minute leaflets

A 'last minute leaflet' is a simple piece of paper distributed on the day before the election, preferably in the evening. It simply reminds people that tomorrow is election day, and that you're the person to vote for. Some people swear by them, others aren't so sure, because it is a hassle getting people to turn out and distribute the ward, just when they thought the campaign was over. Others point out that it reminds everyone when the election is, no matter who they're going to vote for. The contrary argument to that is to distribute last minute leaflets to your 'good' roads only.

It largely depends on how many helpers you have. If there are plenty of bodies, simply rarin' to go, then go ahead. If you're thin on the ground, then a last minute leaflet may be more trouble than its worth.

Posters

There are controversies about posters. Indeed, there have been moves in some parts of the country for the political organisations to get together and agree not to use them. Posters are expensive, they have to be pasted on boards and erected, and householders are increasingly worried that they stimulate vandalism to their property. In fact, it's a very fortunate ward organisation that doesn't have to replace a few which have been torn down overnight – not by political people, but by characters who just get simple-minded pleasure out of doing damage. Nevertheless, posters do have their uses, and the chances are that you will be needing some.

The first thing to realise is that no one ever consciously reads posters. They simply absorb them as they walk or drive past. There is simply no point in trying to get across any sort of complex message. Basically, all you need is your name, your affiliation, and an exhortation to vote for you. Of these elements, your name should have the overriding pride of place. Like so:

Vote
FERGUSON
May 3rd

Some people feel that not even the political affiliation is necessary, relying on the traditional and distinctive party colour to impart that information. Conservatives, especially, tend to feel that way. After all, LABOUR or even DEMOCRAT are fairly short, punchy words, while CONSERVATIVE is long and trooping, and doesn't exactly trip off the tongue.

There is also the problem of *where* to erect your posters, about which, more later.

Window bills

These can be used as a supplement to, or even a replacement for, posters, and very effective they can be, too. The idea is that one of your pieces of literature is designed so that one side of it can be displayed in supporters' windows.

Introduction cards are ideal for this purpose. When your canvassers find a supporter, they can actually suggest that the card they leave behind is used in this way, but even failing that, it's surprising how many people do take the opportunity, even without being asked. After all, it isn't a bad way to ensure that canvassers from other parties don't knock on the door. They have the information they need, displayed in the window.

Other promotional ideas

Budgets usually restrict what a candidate can do, but there is a whole range of other 'selling tools' available to you, and somebody or other is always coming up with something new. Car stickers, lapel badges, balloons are all possible, but quite frankly, they are all a little peripheral. Better to concentrate your resources on the important things. However, if you can manage additional gimmicks, there is no reason why they shouldn't be used. One great advantage of all these things is that they present an image of a lively campaign, encourage your own supporters and helpers, help to start a bandwagon rolling, and sow alarm and despondency in the enemy ranks.

But get the standard things right first.

The imprint

The **imprint** is the line which appears on every piece of election literature, from the largest poster to the smallest lapel badge, stating the name and address of the printer and publisher and it must *not* be forgotten at any price. Any piece of election material that does not bear such an imprint constitutes an 'illegal practice' under electoral law.

In this case, the publisher is your agent, and his address can be that of the campaign headquarters. He'll be very well aware of this, but anyone can make a mistake, and you should always check for yourself. By the same token, it's also worth checking your opposition literature for the same reason. If the imprint has been missed off, then, at the very least, no more of it will be distributed.

YOUR CAMPAIGN BUDGET

No one believes that a millionaire candidate should start with an advantage over someone on income support, so limits are placed on the amount you are allowed to spend on your campaign. And they are strictly observed. If the regulations are breached, then there could be a petition to the High Court and the election could be set aside.

The expenses you are allowed to incur consist of a lump sum, plus a figure for each voter on your own particular electoral roll. The amounts are varied from time to time. As an example, in 1991 candidates were allowed to spend no more than £162, plus 3.2p for every voter. So for a ward with, say, 5,000 names appearing on the electoral roll, a candidate's maximum expenditure was 5,000 x 3.2p = £160 + £162 = £322, which doesn't go far when you're buying print, so such a candidate would probably have spent just about all of it. That gives you a rough idea of the financial implications of your candidacy.

The restrictions are tough to circumvent, too. It doesn't matter if you have a friend in the print trade, willing to do the job for free. He is obliged to state a reasonable price for his services which will show up on the final return of expenses. Even if you don't actually pay him, you can't spend the money you've saved elsewhere. In addition, all payments must be made by yourself or your agent, so no one else can wheel and deal on your behalf. There are petty exceptions, of course. Canvassers, for example, can pay their own bus fares.

The whole matter of expense is complex, and your agent will be very well versed in the intricacies of making returns and associated matters. If you have any doubts, refer to the returning officer.

6
Your Campaign

YOUR ELECTION TEAM

The variety of jobs to be done during an election campaign is far wider than the uninitiated realise. Unless you're very lucky indeed, they can't all be covered by regular members of your ward committee, so you need extra help. Your campaign director will know where to find that help, drawing on experience of previous elections, but as a first-time candidate you will probably be able to call upon family members and friends to lend a hand. It's worthwhile sounding people out as soon as you know you're standing for election, and you could start right now by jotting down some names of people to approach. Here are some notes to help you do that, with spaces for you to enter names if you wish.

Canvassers

Canvassers are the people who circulate the Ward, armed with canvass cards, asking people if they are going to support you. Please note – that's *all* they do. They're not expected to convert anyone on the doorstep. You'll have other people to answer questions – including yourself – although, of course, your thoroughly informed activists could well be members of your canvass team.

This is one of those jobs which quite a few people don't believe they can do. Indeed, some people shy away from it like the plague. It isn't as bad as all that, though: people are much more understanding about such matters than they used to be, and are more forthcoming about their views. Old campaigners will tell you that it's very rare for a voter to be really rude to a canvasser these days, and that, although they don't actually look forward to the job, once they get started, they thoroughly enjoy it.

Of course, you'll be doing more than your fair share of canvassing, and you'll find it's much easier to do so as a candidate than as a helper, because most people want to meet the person they may be

expected to vote for. The more doorsteps you can stand on personally, the better chance you have of winning the election – electors
are more likely to vote for someone they've actually met. The
undecided voters – the ones who decide the result of an election –
may well be swayed if they get a favourable impression of the
candidate who calls on them.

Most experienced campaign directors will tell you that an
experienced canvass team of about six or seven people can cover
an average ward quite adequately, but the more people you have,
the better you can saturate the ward, and the easier the job becomes.

Possibles

....
....
....
....
....
....

Tellers

You'll know that there is usually a representative of each candidate
outside each polling station, taking the electoral registration numbers from people voting. These are the tellers, and unless your own
polling stations are fully covered, you can't know what's going on,
and therefore, where to concentrate your efforts later in the day.
Usually, tellers do one or two-hour stints, but some may attend more
than once during the day.

It's quite a pleasant job, and there usually isn't much difficulty
in finding tellers: a person not quite so agile as he once was, for
example could well find this a useful way to help. It's also a
perfectly acceptable job for a teenager, so perhaps you can rope the
kids in.

Polls are open from 8.00am to 9.00pm, and the first hour or two
is commonly the most difficult period to cover. One answer is for
you to tell yourself at this time. After all, you'll want to be doing
something, and there isn't all that much else to do early in the day.
Also remember that it's a good job for a non-driver. You'll need
your car owners for other purposes. Bear in mind that there may
well be more than one polling station in the same building, with
separate entrances, and that you may need tellers for each.

Possibles

. . . .
. . . .
. . . .
. . . .
. . . .
. . . .

Clerical work

Various jobs arise for people who have a typewriter or word processor at home. The major one is transferring information from canvass returns on to pads which are used on the day, in committee rooms, enabling you to call on known supporters – known as **pledges** – and, hopefully, persuade them to turn out and vote. This can be handwritten, of course, just as long as it's legible.

You will also want to send 'thank you' letters to helpers, and you do that, win, lose or draw, as soon after the election as possible, so it's not too soon to start getting something appropriate drafted out.

Possibles

. . . .
. . . .
. . . .
. . . .
. . . .
. . . .

Poster teams

Erecting posters can be something of a chore. They have to be pasted on to boards, nailed on poles and eventually erected in people's front gardens. In a well-run campaign efforts are made to co-ordinate postering, so that they appear all over the area – not just your Ward – over the same few days, often over the second weekend before election day, so, if you have a large number of poster sites, you may well need more than one team. Supporters with vans, large estate cars, and the requisite tools are vital. No one can do this job on their own – you need two persons per car.

Possibles

....

....

....

....

....

....

Drivers

You can't have too many car drivers on election day – for bringing lists of numbers from polling stations to committee rooms, for 'knocking up' pledges who haven't voted yet, for making sure your tellers get where they're supposed to be on time, and home again afterwards, for driving you around the ward, and generally acting as 'gofers'. You may also need drivers during the campaign period, for getting canvassers around the ward, for example.

Possibles

....

....

....

....

....

....

Literature distribution

Your literature has to be pushed through letter boxes in every house in the ward. Even if the occupiers aren't on the electoral roll, they may be next year. This can be a time-consuming job, and no one wants to 'push out' more streets than they have to. Even before your distributors can start work, the literature has to be sorted into street bundles, in appropriate numbers per street, labelled accordingly, and taken around to your distribution team. You may well have more than one distribution to make during the election period.

If you have time during the day, it's a good job to do yourself. It helps you familiarise yourself with the Ward, and it's no bad thing to be seen working hard around the streets.

Possibles

....

....

....

....

....

....

THE SYSTEM

It would be useful, at this point, to run down the basic campaign system as usually organised. There are variations, of course, from area to area, and organisation to organisation, but the fundamentals are the same, and if you're a stranger to the process, a little background knowledge before you start will come in useful.

In essence, the objectives are to persuade as many people to vote for you as you can, find out who they are, and make sure they get to the polling stations on the day. The 'persuasion' element is usually an integrated affair, co-ordinated by your central organisation, and (in theory, anyway) goes on all year round, rather than just in an election period. The media used during the campaign are literature and posters, and perhaps an overall advertisement in a local newspaper. As far as you, personally, are concerned, you have chances to make your point in local newsletters and in the appropriate sections of your literature.

'Finding out' is the function of the canvass. Voters are approached and quite simply, asked which way their votes are likely to go. Results are entered on canvass cards, by placing ticks against names in columns headed 'F', 'A', 'O', 'D' and 'I' – which stand for 'For', 'Against', 'Doubtful' (which means not that the canvasser is doubtful, but that the voter doesn't know or isn't saying), 'Out' and 'Ineligible'. These results are then transferred to duplicate pads, used on election day to enable your team to 'knock up' pledges.

Election day is devoted to getting as many pledges to the polling station as possible. Tellers take numbers from people who have voted, send them back to the committee rooms, where they are crossed off the duplicate pads. You should, therefore, be able to know, later in the day, where possible votes still remain to be gleaned. You can then send cars to attempt to persuade electors to accept a lift to the polls.

COMMITTEE ROOMS

With that background, you can see that your committee rooms are your headquarters on the day. You need a sizeable room, with space to spread out your duplicate pads and enable helpers to cross numbers off as they come in from the polling stations. You also need a telephone, if not in the room itself, at least somewhere handy. Drivers will be despatched from here, so there needs to be parking space. You should be as close to a polling station as possible. You also need a constant source of tea and coffee!

Ideally, you should be able to operate from just one committee room, but it may be necessary to have a second one somewhere – perhaps because you have widely scattered polling stations, or because your ward is split down the middle by a major road, for example. This is to be avoided if you can, because it complicates matters. Effort is duplicated, and your campaign director can't keep his finger on the pulse of events as efficiently as he would like.

A good committee room should be managed by two people at a maximum. If, during the day, you find people milling about, drinking tea and chatting – then you're doing something wrong. They should be out and about doing things for you.

So now you're all set. Let's get down to the campaign itself.

CANVASSING

Why canvass?

It bears repeating. The only function of your canvass is to find out who's going to vote for you. Canvassers aren't expected to convert anyone on the doorstep – it probably doesn't work anyway.

When to canvass

Roughly speaking, the canvass starts when the campaign does – about four weeks before election day. There may be variations, however, possibly because you have a large Ward and are a bit thin on the ground, which invites you to start a little early. Easter can get in the way too. It isn't considered good form to canvass on a Good Friday, and Easter Monday is an odd day, with many people not at home. For that matter, your canvassers may have other things to do, too. By the same token, Saturdays and Sundays are out.

Canvassing usually starts at about 6.00pm, and goes on until around 8.00 or 8.30. People, especially the elderly, aren't too happy these days about opening their doors to strangers any later than that.

In any case, two hours or so of tramping the streets are enough for most people.

On the other hand, there is a certain amount that can be done during the day. If you have a road, for example, which you know has a high proportion of retired folk, or a specific old people's development, then there's no reason why you can't call on them in the late morning or afternoon. This can make a surprising difference to the time needed for the canvass, because such developments often have dwellings which are very close together, and can therefore be covered more quickly than areas with long drives or front gardens.

Who to canvass

The short answer is 'everyone on the electoral roll'. Of course, that's not really possible, because you can't usually speak to all members of a household.

Often, you'll find that the person you speak to volunteers information. 'Oh yes! I'll vote for you, but you can't count on 'im,' is a reaction most canvassers know well. The assumption is that, in most cases, all members of a household vote alike. This is obviously a dangerous one to make, but it works both ways. If the reaction is favourable, but other family members vote differently, then the same is true when the reaction is unfavourable, and things average out. It's also, obviously, not worth calling on a house displaying an opposition poster or window bill.

It may be, however, that you aren't able to cover the whole ward – you may not have enough help for that, or the weather may intervene. If you have any reason to think that may be so, then concentrate on your 'good' areas first.

There's no point spending too much precious time in streets which you probably won't be knocking up on the day, because there aren't many pledges there. Anyway, why alert the 'antis' to the fact that there's an election on? You'd prefer them to stay at home.

How to canvass

The first thing to realise about canvassing is that it's not something to be afraid of. These days, since the advent of opinion polls and TV saturation coverage of politics, people are a lot more forthcoming about their voting intentions than they used to be, and it's a very rare thing for anyone to be actively rude to you on a doorstep. As a candidate, you'll find it a great deal easier than a helper does. Even if the householder in question is supporting someone else, he's still likely to be interested to meet you.

Before you ring the door bell, look on your canvass card and note the name of the family in residence, and when the door is answered, your approach should be something along the lines of, 'Hallo Mr Jones, I'm so-and-so, your such-and-such candidate at the local election. Can I count on your support?' Hopefully, you'll get a straight 'yes' or 'no' and can tick the appropriate column (preferably out of sight of the voter), and move on to the next house.

Of course, it's frequently not quite as simple as that. People do like to ask questions of the candidates, and most of the time, you'll have ready answers. When you don't, if you're not sure of your ground, don't be tempted to waffle. Quite simply say, 'I don't know. But I'll jolly soon find out and let you know.' Then you *do* find out, and you *do* let the elector know. Remember, however, that your job is to visit as many houses as you possibly can, and try not to get stuck on one doorstep for any longer than you can help. If necessary, arrange to call back. And you should watch out for the occasional political activist who knows perfectly well what you're about, and quite deliberately tries to keep you talking.

You may not get a direct response, one way or another. The rule is to be as tough with your canvass as you can – if you have any doubts at all, put the elector down as an 'against'. In this context, it does no harm at all to be pessimistic. Only if you get a firm 'yes' do you enter a 'for'. It's also worth noting that many people who say something like, 'we'll have to think about it,' are in fact, 'againsts', but don't want to offend you by saying so. Only if you're absolutely sure that the voter genuinely doesn't know which way he's going to vote do you enter a 'doubtful'.

If you don't get a reply to your knock, then that household obviously goes down as an 'out', and if time and available resources permit, call on the 'outs' again. You'll find, however, that if no one comes to the door first time round, then they probably won't at the same time on another evening either. Just to finish with the canvass card, the 'ineligible' column is most commonly used for people who have moved into the area since the electoral register was compiled, and so do not have a vote in your ward on this occasion. It's interesting to make a note of them. You'll be surprised how many 'ineligibles' actually vote on the day. Possibly because the original residents have come back specifically to use their votes.

If you can help it, don't go out on your own. In some areas, campaign managers simply hand over piles of canvass cards at the start of the campaign, and, in effect, say 'come back when you've finished that lot'. This is not to be recommended, however. You have no idea, as the campaign progresses, how well, or badly, you are doing, and the whole process rapidly becomes a boring chore. Much better to meet, at some strategic spot with the team, and descend in a commando raid on a area which your campaign director will have decided upon. That way, you're not on your own, you can swap anecdotes with colleagues, and generally make a fun thing of it. If you're in a 'bad' area, you will appreciate the support, and in a 'good' one, everyone will be cheerful. You're also readily available if a canvasser comes across someone who wants to meet the candidate.

Furthermore, you can finish the evening by having a drink at the local pub, or wherever, and make a social occasion of it.

And, whatever else you do, don't forget to say 'thank you' to the team before you leave them.

Finally, don't forget that all canvass returns must be in the hands of the appropriate helper during the very evening they are obtained. Figures must be worked out and relayed to Central Office, and the information entered on duplicate pads ready for election day as soon as possible. There may also be notes about action your team is required to take – making sure that someone who has requested it is going to be given a lift to the polls at a time convenient to him or her, for example.

A completed canvass card doesn't do anyone any good sitting in a canvasser's handbag for several days.

LITERATURE DISTRIBUTION

Literature has to be pushed through letterboxes in every dwelling in the ward, including those which are displaying opposition posters, because you have no guarantee that every resident is going to vote against you. (This differs from canvassing, where the anti faction is almost bound to answer the door when called upon – Murphy's Law.)

Your campaign director will arrange for your leaflets to be collected from your central organisation, and delivered to the people who are going to bundle them according to the numbers of households listed in the electoral roll for each street. The time scale being what it is, that will probably be done in one evening. Bundles are then distributed to the people who are going to do the actual 'pushing out' – and that includes you.

Obviously, it's a good idea to ask people to deliver around their own areas where possible. You should also be sure that they are given a day by which the job is to be completed, and this is particularly true where you are planning to do more than one distribution. Your distributors should also be told to make sure that all leaflets are pushed right through the letterboxes – for the normal security reasons, but also because some over-keen canvasser from the other side can't then whip it out before the householder has got his hands on it.

Nothing legally stops you from delivering literature on a Sunday, but it is generally reckoned to be bad form to do so. Nevertheless, if you're short of time and help, then you may find yourself forced to do just that – but avoid it if you can.

POSTERING

Posters are the most expensive single item you are likely to use in your campaign. If you are standing as part of an authority-wide team, then your central organisation will be producing them for you, giving you the economies which come with relatively mass production. Often, for example, bulk quantities are produced complete with everything except for your name, which is applied later. Sometimes names are applied by a printer, sometimes they come in the form of stickers to be attached by your own team, either beforehand or while posters are being erected on site.

All right so far, but don't forget that posters have to be mounted on something, usually on rectangles of hardboard nailed to posts, and anyone who is into do-it-yourself knows how expensive such materials can be. In fact, most organisations keep a stock of posts and boards from year to year, and are likely to get a little miffed if they're not returned to some central storage point immediately after the election. There's always some natural wastage; there seems to be a breed of vandal which delights in destroying election posters, and many a householder has discovered that a left-behind post and board makes an excellent tool for sweeping snow from a drive or garden path.

However, the costs involved in postering demand that you use your stock strategically. There's no point in scattering them all over the ward like confetti, siting many where they'll do very little good. So let's start right there.

Where to poster

Any advertising person will tell you that few people ever actually read posters – they just absorb them as they pass by. It is a 'water on a stone' process, depending to a large extent on cumulative effect. So you want to site your posters where most people will see them. Here's a list of the types of site you should be looking for. You'll probably think of others, but this will give you an idea.

Main roads
Commuter routes
Bus routes
Shopping areas
Strategic road junctions
Near well-used meeting places – pubs, community centres etc.
Near polling stations
Near schools – where parents drop and pick up children
Opposite factory gates or large office buildings

There are a couple of exercises you might go through.

- First, take a map of your ward, and mark strategic thorough-fares on it. Then take a trip out around the ward and see for yourself where the best sites are likely to be. Then see how they equate with your 'good' roads – you won't persuade many people to allow you to erect posts on their land if they're not going to vote for you.

- Second, ask your campaign director for a list of poster sites from previous elections, and check with your electoral register that those residents are still living in the appropriate houses. While you are about it, check the list with the pledge list, commonly in the form of a marked-up register, from the last election. You may well find strategically-sited pledges who may be amenable to an approach, but who haven't had a poster before.

Remember, you can't just stick posters up willy-nilly on any old piece of ground you find. They should be on private property with the full permission of the owners. Anything else is 'fly posting' and is an offence.

Poster sites

You may expect that the list of poster sites from previous elections will still be reasonably current, but you can't take it for granted; people move or change their minds, from time to time. So everyone on that list must be checked beforehand, and that includes those at the homes of active committee members. No matter how ardent a supporter may be, there can be circumstances – including fear of vandalism – which may prompt a householder to say 'Sorry, not this year.'

It's a good idea if you can do this checking yourself, because, as a new candidate, you want people to know that you're not taking their support for granted. The more supporters you can call on personally, the better, but there's nothing wrong with using the phone if you have to.

Of course, much of this work can be done as you canvass. Similarly, when you and your team are canvassing a road where you particularly want poster sites, brief your canvassers to ask if you can erect a poster when they come across voters who are firm supporters. It's not sufficient just to identify a house – you also need to locate the spot in which a householder is willing for you to erect a post – nothing offends a gardener more than a pair of dirty great boots trampling all over his prize petunias.

Erection of posters

The dates on which your posters are erected will probably be decided by your central committee, and also by the delivery date promised by the printer. The idea is to create maximum effect by having the whole area suddenly blossom forth with a rash of posters in the appropriate colour. That way, you give the best possible boost to the morale of your helpers and supporters, and spread a little alarm and despondency in the ranks of the opposition at the same time.

The 'due dates' often arrive over a weekend, allowing the work of erection to be done over two full days, and also ensuring that you don't lose any valuable canvassers to the poster teams. This timing also means that there is usually someone at home when your poster team calls, which is helpful, because unless you know the householder very well indeed, you shouldn't just turn up, bang in your post, and leave without talking to someone in residence.

The chances are that you won't have finished your canvass when the postering weekend rolls around, so there's nothing to stop you continuing to look for useful sites after the main operation is complete, even though you will have made sure that your preferred roads have been canvassed before that time. You'll also have to keep an eye on your sites afterwards because you're bound to lose one or two, through the depredations of idiots or the British climate.

LOUDSPEAKERS

You need to think carefully about whether to use a loudspeaker on election day or in the few days leading up to it. Of course, hearing your name blasted into the atmosphere can be a considerable ego boost, but the decibel level can offend people and turn them off you. This is particularly true where people are working nights, or where there are old people's homes or similar establishments. You should also realise that a loudspeaker announcement reminds *everyone* that there is an election on – not just your supporters. If you are defending a big majority, then, statistically speaking, that works in your favour. If you're trying to unseat a sitting councillor, or if things are tight, then – it doesn't.

If you do decide to use a loudspeaker, then insist on writing the script yourself. You need to make just one strong point and that's all; anything else simply confuses things. For example, if you are the only candidate who actually lives in the ward, then something along the lines of 'Your local candidate' can be effective.

THE PRESS

Ignore it. Most local papers have a rule about not giving individual candidates free publicity during a campaign, and indeed, don't particularly want to appear to be politically biassed, one way or another. You might just get yourself a mention in some capacity other than your candidacy, but it's of doubtful value. The difficulty comes on the odd occasion when the press contacts *you*. They're only likely to do so over some contentious issue, and if they do that, then you can bet your life they'll be talking to your opposition as well.

If that happens, don't refuse to talk, or say 'no comment' – that just provokes a story about how you refused to speak on the issue, which looks bad. Much better to say 'I'll get back to you', and consult the appropriate person in your central organisation before you do so. You'll invariably find that there is an agreed 'official' line to take, and anyway, your powers-that-be will certainly want to know that you have been approached, and what your response will be. All in all, it's a bag of worms, during a campaign, and it's better to stay out of it if you can, at least until you have a lot more experience than a new candidate usually does.

Paid advertisements are a different matter. You won't be taking one yourself, because you can't afford it on your allowable expenses, and because you are unlikely to find suitable media for the purpose: there's no point in buying space in a medium which covers the whole town when you're only trying to influence one Ward. However, your central organisation may, on occasion, take advertisement space on behalf of the whole area, and you will be given the opportunity to have an input into that.

The situation with the press also partially explains why the old-fashioned public meeting is a thing of the past, except in special circumstances. They don't get press coverage, and no one comes except your active supporters, anyway. If a 'special circumstance' does arise – the visit of a national figure, for example – then you'll find that you'll have your hand held pretty tightly by your party organisers, and you'll simply do as you're told.

COMPUTERS

All the foregoing relates to the traditional election campaign, which may vary in detail from place to place, but the fundamentals are generally similar.

However, even here, the mighty microchip is beginning to rear its head; many people have experimented with the use of a personal computer to ease the load of the canvassing operation.

But the basics still hold true. *Someone* has to enter the entire electoral register for the Ward into the computer. *Someone* (probably the same someone) has to enter the canvass returns as they come in. *Someone* has to man the committee room on election day and pull the information out of the computer when it is required. Although the whole operation is neater and more sophisticated, it doesn't really save as much time and energy as might at first be expected.

There is also the point that only people who know how to operate computers can be entrusted with any of those jobs, and that is by no means everybody on your team.

However, if you do have such facilities and expertise available to you then go right ahead – and good luck to you.

7
Election Day

Hope you got a good night's sleep, last night, because today is going to be an awfully long one. Most of it will be spent on your feet, so make sure your shoes are comfortable. And it's surprisingly easy to forget to vote yourself, so don't forget to allocate time, and a lift, to take care of that duty.

Polls open at 8.00am, and there's only one job which needs doing at that early stage of the proceedings. All your polling stations must be manned by **tellers** and it's a good idea to do a couple of hours yourself at this period, because you'll be raring to do *something*, and anyway, it's the time of day when it's usually most difficult to find personnel. It can also be a surprisingly busy time of day at the polling stations, because many people like to vote on their way to work, or after dropping the children at school. So let's talk about telling.

TELLING

Your telling operation is absolutely vital, because unless it is carried our efficiently, you won't have much of a clue how things are going, or where to put your efforts in through the day. Asking people if they would mind telling you their registration numbers is straight-forward, because most people carry their polling card with them when they turn up to vote. They don't positively have to, but it does speed things up when they get into the polling station.

You will come across the odd voter who regards his number as private, and won't tell it to you, usually because he doesn't understand the situation, and believes that, somehow or other, you'll be able to find out how he voted. It's nonsense, of course, and can do the voter a disservice, because he's likely to be 'knocked up' later in the day, wasting his time, as well as everyone else's. However, don't press the point. It simply isn't worth getting into a hassle about it. Similarly, if someone asks you why you want his number, simply tell him, 'So that we know you've voted, and won't bother you later in the day.'

The polling station

The areas around the polling station in which you can operate are very restricted. You cannot tell within the precincts of the station itself, but just where those boundaries lie can be a grey area, and, for practical purposes is within the discretion of the officer in charge of the station. This may mean that you're outside in all weathers, but more usually, there is a corridor or vestibule or similar area, which has probably been used for such purposes many times before. And please note, telling is all you can do. You must not hand out literature, or in any other way, seek to influence an elector's vote. About the most active option open to you is to wear a rosette.

As a candidate you are allowed to enter the polling station and talk to the officers in charge, theoretically, to see that everything is satisfactory, which it invariably is. It isn't a bad idea, however, to exercise that privilege and make yourself known to the people in charge. They can be very helpful if any difficulty arises later in the day, and conversely, can make life difficult for tellers, but this is rare. An experienced polling officer knows that tellers can be very useful, in some ways, directing uncertain voters where to go, for example, or making sure that the appropriate notices are visible and don't get blown over by the wind. If you do run into any problems at a polling station, don't try to sort them out yourself. Call in your campaign director. He's had more experience than you.

Finally, strictly speaking, you shouldn't ask people for their numbers on the way into the polling station, but only on the way out – the other way round may be construed as attempting to influence a vote. However, this rule is frequently ignored, partially because tellers can be useful in directing uncertain voters where to go, especially if there is more than one station in the same building. If in doubt, consult the polling officer.

When to start, and when to stop

Your telling operation should be in place and ready to start collecting numbers as soon as the polls open. Knowing when to stop is less clear cut. The primary purpose of all those lists of numbers is to enable you to get supporters who haven't voted to the polling station. This means that the sheets of numbers must be relayed back to the committee room at very regular intervals, the information transferred to duplicate pads, and 'knockers up' despatched. This all takes time, so from this point of view there's no point in telling right up to the moment the polls close – because you won't be able to get 'defaulters' along in time to vote. Just when to pull your telling team out is a judgement best left to your campaign director. He's in a position to see the whole picture, and having rushed about all day, you probably aren't.

In some areas, however, organisations like to have a complete record of voters for statistical purposes, useful for use from year to year. In that case, you may be asked to tell right up to the bitter end, but the practice is of doubtful value.

When to do a stint yourself

There's a school of thought which says the best place for a candidate to be throughout election day is at the polling stations. That's where he'll see, and be seen by, most voters, and anyway, it gets him out of the campaign director's hair. That view is a little extreme, but the principle is sound. If you're not telling, what else are you going to do? You can call on known supporters and make sure they vote, you can drive people who need lifts to the polls, you can do a session or two on a loudspeaker, but you should certainly make sure that you do at least one stint of telling at each polling station in your ward. If you find yourself hanging around the committee room, then something has gone wrong, somewhere. By all means drop in from time to time, encourage the troops, and keep up with how the figures are going, but every moment you spend in that nice, comfortable cocoon, is one when you're not being seen by the people you hope will vote for you.

The figures

All a teller really needs are a supply of paper and a ball-point. However, most organisations supply special pre-printed pads, designed for the purpose. They have a standard number of spaces in which numbers are entered, which makes it easy to check a running total back at the committee room.

Those figures are no use clutched in the hot little hand of a teller. The rule should be that anyone who visits a polling station, for whatever purpose, should see if there are figures to be taken back to the committee room. More – if someone is at a loose end, send him round the stations to pick up figures. It's much better to overdo that particular exercise than to have valuable information lying fallow around the polling stations.

The opposition

Oddly enough, telling is one operation where one can co-operate with the opposition. After all, you're going to be spending a long time with the opposing tellers, and there's very little point in adopting a confrontational attitude. You'll find some of them are quite nice, really.

More to the point, at busy times, you're almost bound to miss a voter or two, and an exchange of numbers with the other people does no harm at all. In at least one Gloucester ward, in the 1980s, both main parties were a little light on tellers, and instituted a carbon-copy system so that both sides kept on top of the job.

By the time you get to election day, all the battle lines are drawn, and apart from getting your own voters out, there's relatively little you can do to influence the result. So why not keep things friendly, to everyone's advantage?

THE COMMITTEE ROOM

By the time you finish your first telling session – about 10.00am – your campaign director will be just about setting up the committee room. Duplicate pads with pledges already entered will be laid out in street order, and helpers will be arriving to start crossing them off as information comes back from the polling stations. There will be a list of times and addresses relating to supporters who need lifts to the polls – some of them identified during canvassing, some 'regulars' from other elections, some from people who have moved away, but who still appear on the register as voters in your ward. Someone will, almost invariably, put a kettle on.

This is your headquarters for the day, and it could well be that you use the same room every year, in which case there is no problem. But let's assume you have to find a new one this year.

Where should it be?

The short answer is – as near to a busy polling station as possible. But that almost invariably means that it's quite a long way from the others. Anyway, you'll find that there are relatively few people both willing and able to tolerate hordes of workers clumping through their house all day, so you must make a value judgement about where the best place for your committee room is.

If at all possible, don't use more than one committee room. That way lies confusion, but if the geography demands that you do so, make sure that one person is firmly in charge at each site. You should also remember that parking space is important, and that cars are going to be buzzing up and down the road all day, so make sure that traffic conditions are suitable. One useful ploy is to use a caravan, if one is available, and simply park it in a supporter's drive for the day. That minimises disruption to the household concerned, and also allows you to set the whole thing up prior to election day. The only problem is that you'll still need a telephone.

Manning the committee room
A committee room full of people is an inefficient one. It's perfectly possible to run the organisation using two people, plus the campaign director when he isn't out and about the Ward.

As numbers come in, one person takes the sheets and calls out the numbers, while the other crosses them off the appropriate duplicate pads. Drivers will arrive at intervals, and will be sent off to knock people up, or deal with lifts. A running total of the figures is kept, and your central organisation will probably want to be kept informed about how the figures are looking.

Things do get more hectic in the evening. You will have more people available, and they must be sent about their business. Figures will be coming in more rapidly than during the day, but, because time is running out, and knocking up is in full swing, they must be entered with the least possible delay. But, nevertheless, people – especially drivers – sitting in the committee room are wasted people, so get them on their way.

Dealing with the figures
Processing the information which arrives from around the ward is one of the two primary functions of a committee room. (The other is acting upon it). Figures from the polling stations make up the bulk of that information, and should be dealt with with the least possible delay. Fundamentally, the system is simple enough:

- The first helper sits down with a telling slip and calls out the first number on the slip.

- The second helper finds the appropriate duplicate pad and looks for the number. If it's there he or she says 'Yes' and crosses it off. If it isn't, the response is 'No'.

- The first helper ticks the 'Yesses' and crosses the 'Noes'.

- When the first slip is complete, the 'Fors' and 'Others' are totted up, and, when that particular pile of slips has been checked, the results are entered on a running total sheet, which should look something like this:

Time	For	Others	Total voted	%For
10.15	78	103	181	43.1
10.45	32	84	116	
	110	187	297	37.0

. . . and so on, throughout the day. It may surprise you to learn that, depending on the accuracy of the original canvass, the candidate in this fictitious example could well be on a winner, in spite of having secured only just over one-third of the votes cast. Remember that the figures only give you the number of pledges which have turned out, compared with everyone else. You have to assume that every candidate is going to get some votes, so if you're not in a two-horse race, there's your first split in the bald statistics. There is also the matter of the 'outs' and 'not sayings', some of whom will have voted for you.

There is a calculation which can be applied here, and it goes back to the canvass returns. Let's assume that your total canvass reveals 1200 pledges, 1000 'againsts' and 1000 others – 'outs', 'don't knows' and 'ineligibles', that's 1200 votes out of a total electorate of 3200, a 'for' percentage of 37.5. However, it is not unreasonable to assume that the people whose votes have not been identified are likely to split in the same proportions as the identified ones – a ratio of 1200 to 1000, or 6 to 5.

In other words, you might expect about 540 of the unidentified votes to come your way, giving you a total potential vote of around 1740 – around 54% of the potential vote. Of course, things aren't quite as rosy as that, and it's unwise to apply that sort of calculation until very late on election day. It may well be that, for reasons of work and geography, most of the opposition voters tend to turn out in the evenings, for example: patterns of voting vary from ward to ward, and a heavy shower of rain at just the wrong time has decided many a close election. This is one reason why it's important to record the time along with your running total: your campaign director will be able to compare figures with the same time of day last time around, and have a fair idea how things are going.

Deploying the troops

Many of us gained our first experience of electioneering as small boys on bicycles. The idea was that we would spend the day pedalling like mad between polling stations and committee room with lists of numbers – rather as Joris and company brought the good news from Ghent to Aix. The advent of the generally-available motor car has diminished that job, these days, but it's still a perfectly useful thing for a young family member to do during the day.

Some of the troops will have been deployed before the big day dawns, of course. The telling roster will have been settled days ago, for example. But there never was an election campaign yet where something didn't go wrong. A family crisis can suddenly force Mrs Bloggins to withdraw from her stint sitting outside the polling station, and you have to find a replacement immediately. For this reason, it's useful to have a couple of car drivers available to shoot off and mend the damage, in between picking up voters and collecting telling slips.

As the day wears on, 'knocking up' becomes more and more the major preoccupation, and you may well find that your campaign director will spend most of the evening in the committee room sending out teams for that purpose. It's as well to have some idea beforehand about which roads you want to knock up at what times of the day, although your ideas on that will change as events develop. There's little use, for example, knocking up half-a-dozen houses in a plum road, while the residents of another have hardly turned out at all.

It's waste of manpower to use drivers with available cars for telling or committee room duty in the evening. Much better to have them out on the road harvesting your votes.

KNOCKING UP

'Knocking up' is the time-honoured practice of calling on pledges who haven't voted yet, reminding them that it's election day, persuading them to turn out, and offering them lifts to the polls and back. No one likes the job very much, and there is a school of thought which denies that it does much good. The answer to that is that no one really knows how effective knocking up is, because relatively few voters accept the offer and turn out then and there. However, inspection of electoral registers afterwards does seem to indicate that voters do tend to turn out in larger numbers after a knocking up operation, and if you lose by a handful of votes, you'll probably say to yourself, 'If only we'd done more knocking up!'

When to knock up
Most of the knocking up operation goes on in the evening. That's when you have enough figures to know where you should be putting in your effort, when most people are at home, and when you have most drivers available. However, there's nothing to stop you mounting the odd commando raid at any time of the day. Indeed, sometimes it can be highly effective. One example of this is the situation where you have a housing development designed for retired folk, who are therefore home all day. A couple of cars can glean a significant number of votes in such cases, often driving voters to the polls, and then into town for shopping afterwards, saving the elector a bus fare and a tiring journey.

Don't make this sort of a foray too early, though. Senior citizens often value their lie in of a morning, or prefer to potter around in dressing gowns with cups of tea at the ready. And who can blame them? However, this is one aspect of the campaign you can plan beforehand. Why not do it now?

EARLY KNOCK UPS

Street/area	Time	Polling Station
. . . .	. . . .	. . . .
. . . .	. . . .	. . . .
. . . .	. . . .	. . . .
. . . .	. . . .	. . . .

Where to knock up
Start with your best roads and work your way downwards. That's a simple enough concept, but it may be influenced by voting patterns. In practice, you'll find that the sheets from duplicate pads which have the smallest number of pledges indicated as having already voted are the ones to concentrate on. Both factors must be taken into consideration, and an experienced campaign director soon develops a 'gut feel' about the matter.

How to knock up
It's quite possible for a helper to arrive at a chosen street, park his car, knock on doors, and give anyone a lift who asks for it. If your resources are stretched, then that's what you might have to do.

However, there are more efficient ways of setting about things. Possibly the most common of these is for two people to set out in one car and take one side of the road each. The number of people who actually avail themselves of the offered lift is small enough for one car to be used quite efficiently in this way, and you cover the road much faster. For that matter, it's fairly usual for three people to descend on a road with two cars; that way someone is always door knocking, and there is always a car available for a lift.

When you arrive on a doorstep, armed with your duplicate slip from the committee room, the preferred approach is to say 'Good evening Mr So-and-So. Just calling to remind you it's election day. Would you like a lift to the polling station?' What happens then depends on the reply you get. Here are some typical versicles and responses:

'Oh yes! So it is. We'll be along later.'
'Thanks very much! Would you like us to send a car for you? What time?
'No thanks! We can get there under our own steam.'
'Great! We'll look out for you.'

(This voter may or may not have any intention of coming along, but the response is often quite genuine, and a later check will reveal that a surprising number of voters really do turn up after such a call.)

'Oh, I'd forgotten. Don't think I'll bother this year.'
'Well – we do need your vote, and we have a car right here for you. Or would you like us to send it back later?'

(If the voter genuinely has forgotten it's election day, then this approach can work well. But it does depend on what's on the telly that night.)

'No. I'm not coming. Too tired/can't be bothered'
'I'm sorry about that, but thanks for your support anyway'

(There's no point in wasting time. You won't persuade him anyway.)

'I've already been.'
'Oh – very sorry to have bothered you. Thanks for your support.'

(He could have slipped through the net at the polling station, or refused to give his number. Or he may have voted in the interval before his number was relayed to the committee room. On the other hand, he may be telling lies to avoid having to turn out. Either way, there's no point in hanging about.)

> *'Oh yes! Just wait until I get my coat on!'*
> 'Fine! I'll get the car.'

(This is the best of all, of course, but you'll find it isn't all that common. But don't get discouraged. Even a couple of dozen votes garnered by the knocking up operation can swing a local election.)

THE COUNT

During the last few days of the campaign, you'll receive a letter from the returning officer enclosing a piece of paper which admits you to the count. Candidate or not, you won't get in without it, so for goodness sake don't forget it. The same applies to your guests and counting agents. The covering letter will also ask you to be present at the count as soon after 9.00pm as possible, to avoid too much toing and froing while people are trying to count. No doubt, as a first time candidate, you'll want to do just that, especially if you've never attended a count before. It's only fair to warn you, however, that the first hour or so of any count is frankly boring. The boxes containing the ballot papers have to arrive, be unsealed and opened, and then the papers have to be counted just to see that there are precisely the same number as stated by the officers who have manned the polling station all day. That all takes time, and doesn't yield any interesting spectacle.

It does give you time to look around, however. You'll find that yours is probably not the only Ward being counted in that particular room, and that, therefore, you'll have a chance to compare notes with colleagues standing in other Wards. You can also say 'thanks' to your guests and counting agents, and also 'make your number' with the deputy returning officer controlling your own count. Your own central agent will probably be along to say 'good luck', and he may well have a better idea how your day has gone than you have, because he will have been receiving regular bulletins throughout the day from your committee room.

As anyone who has ever watched a count on television knows, the counting takes place along one long table. On one side sit the people who actually count the ballot papers, on the other the counting agents representing each candidate. The deputy returning officer normally presides from the head of the table.

As boxes are emptied, bundles of papers are distributed among the counters, who arrange them in bundles of 50 – at this point there is no attempt to split them among the various candidates. When the total number of votes has been reconciled with the information relayed by the polling officers, the count proper can begin. And that's when the fun starts.

Now's the time when the votes are split between the various candidates. The bundles of 50 ballot papers are taken and divided appropriately, and again sorted into bundles of 50, each one for a single candidate. As each bundle is prepared, it is laid out on the table in a row assigned to that particular person. Usually, there are cards at the head of the table, identifying each row. By this method, you can tell immediately where you stand in the race, and by remembering that each bundle contains 50 votes, can have a good idea of exactly how many votes are coming your way. If things are close, this can become very tense, with one row of bundles edging ahead of the others, and then being caught again.

Here's where it pays to know your ward. By identifying the ballot box being emptied at the moment, you know which polling station it comes from. If that station serves a 'bad' area of the ward, then you won't expect many votes from it – and vice versa.

The returning officer

The returning officer is the seat of all power at a count. Usually the chief executive officer of the authority, his is the final voice on all matters, he makes all the decisions and adjudicates on any controversy. His word is law. He is assisted by deputy returning officers for each ward, who are often senior officers of the Council, and preside at the head of the table at each count. They also announce the result for their ward, proclaiming the total number of votes cast, the numbers cast for each candidate, and the number of spoiled papers.

They also ensure that everything is done according to the proper form, that no one does anything they shouldn't, and make the first decision over whether a particular paper is spoiled or not – and that can lead to argument.

Counting Agents and guests

Your counting agents are the people who sit at one side of the table and look after your interests. They watch the votes being counted with eagle eyes, and try to make sure that none of your votes get into another candidate's pile, and also check that all bundles do, in fact, contain 50 votes, no more and no less. You usually have three of such agents, but this does depend, to some extent, on the number of candidates standing in your ward. There has to be room at the table for all of them, after all.

Guests simply watch proceedings. Again, the amount of room available, and the layout of the rooms where the count takes place, decide the number of guests you can invite. Quite often they will find themselves sitting on a public gallery somewhere, and may not even be able to see the action at the ward they are particularly interested in. In such circumstances, however, grapevines are remarkably efficient, and news does get back to the guests as things progress.

It's entirely up to you to decide who you invite to attend. Obviously, your family will want to have a say in the matter, and sometimes special arrangements are made for spouses and partners. It's also a good way to say 'thanks' to people who have worked particularly hard for you. Do give some careful thought, however, to the people you ask to act as your counting agents. If you have someone who has done the job before, then he or she should be your first choice. If not, ask someone young, enthusiastic and keen-eyed. Often, your campaign director will fill the bill. This is no place for a sentimental attachment to anyone who 'can't be left out'. He can.

Spoiled papers

The two basic rules about a ballot paper is that the voter's intention must be clear, and that there must be no means of identifying him or her. This means that the traditional cross is not the only way in which a vote can be cast. The appropriate name can be ticked, or indicated by any other mark, as long as it's not a signature or a set of initials which might lead someone to be able to identify the elector. On one occasion at least, the phrase 'Good luck!' written alongside one candidate's name has been deemed to make the voter's intention absolutely clear, and the vote therefore accepted as valid.

A ballot paper may also be regarded as spoiled 'for want of the official mark', which is very hard, because it isn't the elector's fault. This mark is a pattern of perforations punched into each paper as it is handed to the voter. Sometimes, if things are hectic, one or more of the perforations does not pierce the paper, and the vote is then invalid. This is something your counting agents will be looking out for.

Spoiled papers can lead to a lot of argument, involving returning officers, candidates, agents and counting agents, and they usually arise around whether the voter's intention is clear or not. If, for example, an elector has actually crossed out every name on the ballot paper but one, and has made no other mark, then it could be argued that he intended to vote for the candidate whose name he left intact. On the other hand, the opposition candidate could contend that there is no positive mark to indicate that the intention was to vote for that particular opponent. Spoiled papers are displayed at one end of the table where candidates can inspect them at their leisure.

Recounts

If the votes are – in your opinion – close enough to warrant it, you can claim a recount. If the returning officer agrees (and he will, unless you're being unreasonable), then all or part of the counting process is repeated. Almost invariably, the second count will differ from the first one, by a vote or two, and the chances are that another recount is requested. This process can go on for hours.

It is your decision, but your heart will be thumping a bit at this point, and your judgement may not be sound. Much better to call the Agent in and be guided by him. In effect, let him take over. As a rule of thumb, remember that there are 50 votes in a bundle. Any majority above that means that more than one bundle has to be incorrect for a recount to have any chance of succeeding. Having said that, there are many cases where a bundle has been found to have fallen under the table, so it's worth taking a look around the floor if things are close.

If votes are level, then you'll have several recounts, and if you can't be separated, then the returning officer will call upon you to decide by **lot**. This can take any form, usually by drawing slips of paper from a ballot box, but sometimes an actual toss of a coin. Either way, it's quite the worst way to win – and an even worse way to lose.

Watching proceedings

As a candidate, you can spend your time wandering around the table and watching proceedings. If you think you spot something wrong, then alert a counting agent, or tell the deputy returning officer. You are not allowed to take part in the action in any way at all, and must not touch a ballot paper. Do remember, that you are the only person allowed to stroll about in this way. Guests can't.

The result

You may be able to see the result comparatively quickly, or you may be on a cliffhanger. Either way, at the conclusion of the count, the deputy returning officer will call candidates together and read the result to them. This is the point where, if necessary, you can ask for a recount. After that, the deputy returning officer will go to a microphone and announce the result, and you'll immediately find that you are surrounded by supporters, giving congratulations or commiserations.

Win or lose, you will probably find a sense of relief. It's all over at last. Until next time.

AFTER THE COUNT

You've either won or you've lost. Either way, your first priority is to thank all the people who helped you and voted for you. Just how you accomplish that depends on your resources and the type of help you received from particular people. For example:

'Thank you' letters

With a little ingenuity, you can make one letter applicable to just about everyone, whether you won or lost. Here's a suggestion:

> Dear
>
> I'm writing to offer you my sincere thanks for your invaluable help during the Election. If ever I can return the favour, in any way at all, please don't hesitate to get in touch.
>
> Personally, I thought the result was an excellent one from several points of view, and we can only go from strength to strength in the future. It's just not possible to fight such an Election vigorously without such assistance, and yours was greatly appreciated.
>
> Best wishes
>
> Sincerely,

The best thing to do is to have the body of the letter reproduced and then add the salutation and subscription in your own handwriting. Use first names where you can. And get the letters out quickly. Send them to tellers, people who offered poster sites – just about everyone, really.

You'll also want to thank the electors in your ward who voted for you, and the traditional letter to the press is still about the best way to do that:

The Editor, 'Bilberry Advertiser'

Sir,

I would be grateful if you would allow me some of
your valuable space to thank all those voters of High
Street Ward who supported me in the recent Council
Election. I considered the result to be an excellent
one, and I do appreciate the excellent support I
received from all parts of the Ward. Thanks
everyone!

   Yours faithfully,

   Joan Smith
   . . . . . . Candidate, High Street Ward.

Please note, you can claim the result as an excellent one whether you won or lost. It will stiffen support next time round.

Have a party!

Nothing extravagant: just a little cheese and wine for the dozen or so most active helpers and their partners. This would include ward committee members, your most energetic canvassers and anyone who worked harder than most. Quite often, such a 'thank you' can be held immediately following the next scheduled meeting of the Ward Committee.

'Thank you' stickers

You will want to get your posters down and away as soon as possible, but as elections are held on Thursdays, the chances are that that won't be until the weekend. If you have the energy, and can afford it, a simple THANK YOU sticker, applied across the posters will attract a lot of attention. Do it on Friday, and take the posters down on Sunday. In parliamentary elections you will often find that this exercise is actually accomplished on election night, following the count. If you can do it – why not?

Finally, do remember that you'll probably need the help of all those people at the next election. Or if you don't, someone else will.

WINNERS AND LOSERS

No one ever said it better than Rudyard Kipling:

> *If you can meet with Triumph and Disaster*
> *And treat those two imposters both the same ...*

If you've won, you'll be filled with euphoria, and that will persist for some days. People start calling you 'Councillor', which makes you feel good, and letters start arriving addressed that way. Indeed, on the day following the election you'll probably receive a large brown envelope, packed with goodies such as the book containing the Council's standing orders, details about allowances and expenses, and similar pieces of information which you'll be required to assimilate. That euphoria does fade when you actually start working, but you'll never quite lose the sense of pride which comes with 'fighting the good fight' and winning.

If you've lost, then you'll be disappointed, but that doesn't last long, because nothing has actually changed, and you'll go about your life much as you always did. However, almost invariably, you'll have acquired a taste for it and will want to have another go. Fighting an election as a candidate is a highly enjoyable experience, and you'll always be able to say you've done it.

Today's losers – tomorrow's winners
And vice versa. Many a highly successful councillor has lost his first couple of elections, but has acquired a steadily rising vote as a consequence. Eventually, the tide turns. Conversely, many a councillor has suffered the reverse experience, often through no fault of his own. One of the oldest truisms in local politics is that 'you can't buck a national swing'. In 1990 a large number of Conservative councillors lost their seats simply because of the unpopularity of the poll tax, which really had nothing to do with them. Similarly, many Labour supporters and Social Democrats

won seats which, only months before, would have been regarded as lost causes.

Keep on keeping on

Never give up. Remember, there are wards other than the one you fought, and you could well find that, next time, such wards will approach you. Make it known that you wouldn't be averse to such an approach, and keep active in your local organisation.

If you are now a sitting councillor, remember that laurels are for winning, not resting on. About the most common criticism which a councillor hears is 'we never see them except at election time'. It's almost invariably not true, and you can't be everywhere at once, but do everything you can to maintain a high profile – in the Council chamber and outside.

Winner or loser – well done, and best of luck!

8
The New Councillor

All right, so you've won an election. But you're not quite a councillor yet, even though supporters will be addressing you by that title as soon as, or even before, the result is officially announced. Technically speaking, you are not a Member of a local authority until you have signed a **Declaration of Acceptance of Office**. Often, the returning officer, or one of his helpers, will lead you firmly to a big book designed for the purpose and invite you to sign on the appropriate dotted line. In other places you'll be asked to drop in to see the chief executive of your authority for that purpose, sometime in the first few days after your election. Cutting it a bit fine, some authorities bring the book along to early meetings of the council and get new Members to sign before they actually sit down. But the document does have to be signed before you can take any action as a councillor.

CHOOSING COMMITTEES

Committees available will vary from council to council, and according to which type of local authority you are now a member of. Education, for example, is a responsibility of county councils, while district councils covering the same areas are the homelessness authorities and will have a housing committee. With wide changes in local government in the offing, it's impossible to be specific about this at the present time – by the time you read this, you may be a member of a **unitary authority** rather than one under the two or three-tier system which has been in operation since 1973.

However, you'll be very well aware of the situation in your area even before you start campaigning, and may have stated your interests and the committees you intend to sit on as part of your election address. Whether you can comply with that statement is another matter entirely.

Your group leader will be wanting to sort his committee representation out as soon as he can, and will give you a piece of paper listing all the major committees and sub committees, and ask you to indicate your preferences. That's simple enough, but you do need to know how many such bodies you will be able, or required, to sit on before you can do that. This you can work out for yourself.

How many committees?

Normally, you can expect the political make-up of the committees to reflect the constitution of the Council – if your party or organisation has exactly half the Council's membership, then you can expect exactly half the seats on each committee, to take the easiest example. Unfortunately things don't usually work themselves out that simply. Here's the process:

1. Take the number of members your party has on the full council.
2. Divide by the total council membership. That gives you the fraction of seats available to your party.
3. Look in the *Council Handbook*, a copy of which you will have been given by now, and tot up the number of committee and major sub committee seats available.
4. Multiply by the fraction obtained, and that gives you the total number of seats available to your party.
5. Divide that by the number of members you have, and you'll have a guide to the number of committees you should serve on.

Example

Number of party members	12
Council membership	32
Divide	3/8
Total number of seats available	112
Apply the fraction	42
Divide by number of party members	$3^1/_2$

You obviously can't have half a seat, so you will probably be asked to sit on either three or four committees.

Sometimes, of course, the politics of the situation can confuse this system, particularly if the numbers representing each party approach parity. In that case, everyone will be out to poach the odd seat so as to increase their voting strength, and the matter will be resolved at the council's Annual Meeting.

Which committees should you choose?

As a new member, you probably won't get exactly what you want – your more senior and experienced colleagues will be given preference. Nevertheless, there are factors you should take into account when making your selection. If you happen to be a builder by trade, for example, you may wish to use your expertise by sitting on – say – planning or housing committees. But think carefully. If your company works, or is likely to work, for your own local authority to any marked degree, then you may find yourself having to declare a financial interest on too many occasions for comfort, and that can deprive your group of both your vote and your voice.

Committee structure varies from council to council, in both substance and terminology. One authority's policy and resources committee can be another's finance and general purposes committee, policy and finance, or whatever. That same committee may, for example, allocate grants to outside bodies, while another council may have a special body for that purpose. It's therefore impossible to be absolutely specific in any advice on the matter. However, here are some pointers:

Policy
Whatever it's called, this is the king-pin committee which reviews the work of all other committees, gives permission for budget money to be spent, and generally sets the policy for the whole authority. It often has more members than the other programme committees, and usually has seats for the Chairmen of all the bodies. Obviously, competition for seats is intense, and you're not very likely to gain one in your first term. If you do get a chance, however, take one.

It's the best vantage point from which to get an overview of the whole scene. One word of warning: meetings tend to be lengthy.

Housing
You might be surprised to find that more experienced members are very ready to step aside in your favour when it comes to housing. On the face of it, it's a good committee to join, because housing problems are very common, cause a great deal of misery, and are just the sort of thing you would like to get your teeth into. Full housing committees, however, aren't quite what most people imagine them to be. There's a great deal of figure work, a whole textbook's worth of technicalities, and a general air of not being able to achieve what one would like to.

It's a good training ground, however, and although it's a 'difficult' committee for a new member, you do learn a lot very quickly. But be prepared to be bored, unless you have a genuine burning interest in the subject.

Planning

If you can get on to the planning committee, do so. There's no better place from which to learn what is likely to happen in your locality, or give you advance warning of important or contentious issues. Again, there are a lot of technicalities, but they're ones you're going to have to learn anyway.

Decisions made by planning committees are very frequently the end of the matter, and can't be overturned by full council. This is particularly true of planning consents – an applicant shouldn't be kept waiting for a decision any longer than is necessary. If you do find yourself a seat, be prepared to be lobbied, and your influence sought by everyone from the chap who wants to build an extension on his house, to the pressure group who wants to preserve an ancient building.

Public Works

This may be called 'technical services' or something similar, these days, and is sometimes combined with the planning committee, but whatever your authority's system, this particular function is one with which you'll wish to become involved. Everyone wants a hole in the road mended at some time, needs a few extra street lamps, wants something done about a traffic problem, or something similar, and you would do well to put yourself in the best position to help out. It's the 'nitty gritty' body, and membership can give you a great deal of influence.

Leisure

There's always a great deal of competition to serve on leisure services committees for fairly obvious reasons. They also tend to have less political controversy than others. In addition, almost everyone has some experience which is useful – perhaps you play football, have an interest in local history, enjoy music, or whatever.

Although leisure budgets tend to be high, there is never enough money to do everything you would like, and part of the expertise is learning where resources should be allocated to do the most good. It would be true to say that leisure committee members have most fun – and there's nothing wrong with a Councillor enjoying his work. But you must be prepared to be frustrated.

Personnel
Unless you have special experience – as a trades union officer or an employer, perhaps – the committee or sub committee which looks after the welfare and interests of the council workforce is one to avoid as a new councillor. Again, the technicalities are prodigious, and the learning curve very steep. Most conditions of employment are decided at national level, but most authorities have some local agreements, and interpretations can vary widely. Personnel committees tend to have 'spin off' bodies which allow members to talk directly with staff representatives, or hear appeals against grading decisions or on disciplinary matters, so the thing can be time consuming. Staff can usually expect to take part in such meetings in their normal working hours, so there can be numerous daytime meetings too.

Environmental Services
This is possibly the most useful committee for a new councillor to serve on, simply because the sheer variety of issues covered offers very wide experience.

An environmental services committee may deal with street cleaning and refuse collection, environmental health matters, including inspection of food premises, public entertainment and other licences, cemeteries and crematoria, hackney carriages, markets . . . in fact, it sometimes seems that if a topic doesn't fit comfortably anywhere else, environmental services gets it. Politics tend to be minimised.

Privatisation
The various pieces of government legislation which seek to introduce competition into local government have added a new factor to the whole system. In many places the councils' own workforces have won contracts for various services, which means that councillors can find themselves on opposite sides of the fence on occasion. For example, if the workforce has won the street cleaning contract, then there will be a body to oversee the 'direct labour organisation' so formed.

The council's interests will be served by one of the programme committees, which becomes a 'client' committee. It's a bit difficult to serve on both.

SUB COMMITTEES AND OTHER ANIMALS

Of course, council life doesn't end with the major committees.

You'll find that most of them have sub committees to deal with ongoing functions – licensing and grants, for example – and there may be working parties which consider various *ad hoc* matters, such as pedestrianisation of a particular shopping centre, perhaps. There is also a whole raft of outside bodies which have council representation on their controlling committees. You'll be expected to do your bit in this respect, and it's fatally easy to find yourself involved with more than you can reasonably handle. Be careful to pick organisations in which you have a genuine interest, and ones to which you can get along reasonably easily.

MEETING PEOPLE

If you intend to be a thoroughly effective councillor as soon as possible, then you can't start making yourself known to people too early. As a new councillor, you may not even know members of your own group at all well, but that soon resolves itself in the natural order of events. It's also worth meeting important members of your opposition as soon as you can, because you'll find that many things you discuss, and activities in which you take part, don't have a political dimension at all – in fact, for practical purposes, you're on the same side. You'll have to play this one by ear, depending on the situation and upon the personalities involved. However, there's nothing to stop you going up to someone you don't know and saying, 'Hello, I'm John Smith. Who are you?' You may be surprised at what reasonable people some of your opponents turn out to be.

Officers
You should certainly get to know as many officers of the council as soon as you can. Chief officers are usually no problem, because they are always in evidence at meetings, but a great many very useful people don't attend committees, and you should seek to arrive on the same wavelength as them as soon as you can.

It's very handy, for example, to be on good terms with the chap who actually organises council house repairs – it can short-circuit a great deal of bureaucracy.

As soon as you know your committees, ring the chief officers concerned, and arrange to visit their departments. They'll be happy to show you round, because they need your goodwill as much as you need theirs. That will enable you to identify the lower-tier officers likely to be of particular use to you.

And never underestimate the power of a chief officer's secretary.

She can do a lot to make sure that her boss really does do what he's promised.

STANDING ORDERS AND PROCEDURE

You really must take time to mug up on the council's standing orders – the rules by which the authority runs its affairs. A thorough knowledge of these can make life much easier, prevent you making a fool of yourself, and enable you to achieve things by the most expeditious route. This is particularly true of rules of debate. One hoary old ploy, for example, can be brought into play if the Chief Executive Officer, the final arbiter on all such matters, rules that such-and-such a subject is out of order, and cannot be discussed.

There's nothing you can do about that, but conversely, he can't stop you standing up and saying 'I'm sorry the Chief Executive has ruled in this way, if he hadn't, I would have said . . . ' You then go on and make your speech, ending with the words, 'However, the Chief Executive says I can't say that, so I won't.'

You'll find that the Member who is a master of procedure can get away with murder, and why shouldn't it be you?

GET ON YOUR FEET

Most of us have an in built reluctance to stand up and speak before sizeable gatherings, but it's an antipathy you're going to have to conquer. Committee meetings tend to be reasonably informal, and don't present too much of a problem, but full council can be very intimidating for the new-comer. The answer is to get on your feet and say *something* as soon as you possibly can, because the longer you leave it, the more difficult it gets.

A good group leader will know this perfectly well, and will give you a specific job to do at your first council, but he won't expect you to set the world on fire, first time round. From your own long-term point of view, it doesn't really matter if you make a hash of it: the ice will be broken, and you'll do better next time. Many a green councillor who has been absolutely crucified on his first entry into debate has become a formidable opponent as a result of the experience.

COPING WITH DIVIDED LOYALTIES

Right from day one you will be faced with the old dilemma – where do your first loyalties lie in case of conflict? To your constituents, who voted you in? To your party or organisation who worked for you, and possibly provided some of the finance? To the authority of which you are a member – which is really another way of saying to the larger area of which your ward is a part?

Everyone, except some very active politicians, would agree that the party comes last in this list. There isn't such a consensus about the other two. Some people consider that your constituents should hold your first loyalty, specifically because a majority of them voted for you precisely to safeguard their interests, and everyone else should be secondary to your thinking. Others would contend that the larger constituency represented by the Council should have your allegiance, because what is good for the whole authority should be good for your ward in the larger scheme of things. And anyway, you're not a delegate, you're a representative.

One wouldn't want to allow this old problem to be taken out of perspective. Most of the time, the matters you consider will be wide enough in their implications so that you can take the broader view, and the decisions you make have authority-wide implications. Only where your ward and your ward only, is affected need you have a real problem. But such occasions do arise, and the conflict does have to be resolved.

Reconciling the conflict

Two factors invariably exist which help if you find yourself split between ward and authority.

- The first is that you are all in the same boat. Your colleagues will completely understand your situation, and your own group will try to help you out. So will the Council officers.

- The second is that these things don't suddenly blow up out of the blue: there is usually time to seek a compromise that will satisfy everyone. If such an accommodation does not prove to be possible, then you must vote the way your own conscience tells you to, and seek some sort of damage limitation afterwards.

More difficult, often, are the occasions when the interests of your ward conflict with those of your group. That particular battle is usually fought behind closed doors at group meetings, so that a united front is presented to the council. Again, you will have the understanding of your colleagues, and the time in which to resolve the matter. The important thing is that your group isn't taken by surprise at the council meeting. You should make sure that your feelings are well known to colleagues at group level: if they know you feel bound to oppose them, then they can act accordingly.

You may have the option of abstaining from a vote, but if the various voting strengths are evenly matched, you may be almost as unpopular for that as if you had actually voted against your group. If it comes down to the bottom line, the interests of your constituents must take precedence over those of your group.

Confidentiality

You will inevitably come into possession of confidential information, and sometimes it will affect the interests of your ward. The temptation to spill the beans can be very strong indeed, but it must be resisted. Confidentiality should only ever be imposed for very good reasons – the figures involved when considering tenders for contracts, for example. Eventually, all will be revealed, and you can act accordingly at that time. If you feel that such confidentiality is unjustified, then raise some quiet hell behind the scenes, with Chairpersons, other members, at your group level and with the appropriate officers. But don't go rushing to the press.

Interests

The other sort of conflict is where a council decision may be against your own financial or personal interest. This isn't a situation to play ducks and drakes with, and the rule is quite simple: declare your interest at the appropriate meeting, leave the chamber if necessary (it isn't, always), and take no part in that particular debate. Even where your interest is remote, it's better to play safe and declare it. After all, legal penalties for non-declaration are severe.

In cases where the interest is indirect – if it affects a close family member rather than yourself, for example – there is a procedure which helps. You can apply to the Secretary of State for a **dispensation**. This isn't as complex or as heavy-handed as it sounds, and your Chief Executive Officer will be able to do the job for you over the phone, possibly in minutes. Such a dispensation may enable you to speak and vote on the issue, or may just allow you to speak. Again, make sure your group knows, in advance, that you have such an interest. To repeat, if in doubt – declare your interest.

HOLDING ON TO YOUR SEAT

One of your major preoccupations, right from the start, should be to make sure that you can hold the seat next time round. Even if you decide not to stand again yourself, you'll want your seat to be filled by someone of whom you approve. The basic principle is to do all you can to let all your voters know what you are doing, trumpet your successes and minimise your inevitable failures. Your ward organisation will see this just the same way, and will do everything they can to make the seat safe.

Working with the press
You'll find that you have a great deal more leverage as a councillor than as a mere candidate. This is particularly true of dealings with your local press. Anything you say may be written down and given in evidence, and it is up to you to see that such writings reflect in your favour. All that really needs is practice, and you'll rapidly develop an instinct for such matters. The basic requirement is for you to be sensitive to opportunities as they arise: to make yourself aware of the sort of issue which your own local media like to cover, and see that they know your opinions on such matters.

There is usually a press table provided at both committee and full council meetings, so you won't find it difficult to identify your local journalists. But, at the beginning, they won't know you, so stroll over at the beginning or the end of the meeting and make yourself known to them. Make sure they have your telephone number, and can rely on you to make a comment, so long as no issues of confidentiality are involved.

When you are to make an important speech which you have prepared beforehand, see that a copy is placed on the press table, before or after the meeting. After all, pressmen are only human, and if they don't have to make copious shorthand notes, then you are much more likely to find yourself quoted in tomorrow's newspaper.

It's also as well to make sure that the attending journalists know what's going on. They're probably not specialists on local government, as you are, may not understand procedure or technicalities, and, in any case, won't have the background knowledge that you do. You'll find that a quiet word of explanation at the right time will be much appreciated and will pay dividends as far as you are concerned. Above all, don't be afraid of the press. They're doing a job, just the same as you are.

Holding surgeries
Many councillors like to run regular **surgeries**, at some meeting place within the ward, where constituents can come to you with their problems and requirements. There's a lot to be said for this

custom, but don't expect long queues of people clamouring for your help. Unless some enormous issue is occupying the minds of a great number of voters – as happened with the Poll Tax in 1990 – enquiries at such surgeries tend to be sparse.

But that's not the point. The important thing is that you are making yourself available to your constituents, and are seen to be doing so. Publicise your surgeries by any means you can: mentions in your ward newsletters, notices on appropriate notice boards, and in the windows of friendly shopkeepers, for example. Please note, you're not being political at this point; you're acting as an energetic local representative.

Newsletters

Your ward organisation will be distributing newsletters around the ward at frequent intervals, and will probably encourage you to keep the editor informed about your recent activities. They will certainly bear your address and telephone number. While you may wish to make a point or two about major issues within the authority, the ward newsletter is an ideal platform for the multitude of parochial matters which arise. For example:

We've been getting complaints about difficulties older people are having crossing the road at the junction of Broad Street and High Street. Councillor Joan Smith has taken the matter up with the City Engineer, and has asked for a pedestrian island to be erected in the road at this point. She is also taking up the matter of badly needed traffic lights outside the supermarket.

9
Committee Work and Debate

FULL COUNCIL – THE LARGEST COMMITTEE

Almost certainly, the first meeting you are summoned to attend will be a full council meeting. In fact, it will be the statutory Annual Meeting of the council, the main business of which is to appoint committees for the ensuing year, and elect the chairs of those bodies. The very first such chair to be decided will be the most important one of all – the Chairman of the Council, who in the case of District Councils may well be the Mayor. This means that, in many towns and cities, the first part of the annual meeting of Council is the traditional Mayor-making ceremony, with its robes, chains and macebearers.

In such cases, that's when you really know you're a councillor; a link in a chain which may well stretch back for centuries. In a relatively few cases, these days, the ceremony will also include the election and appointment of a **Sheriff**, who may or may not be the vice chair of the Council. After the tradition is over, the meeting will proceed to appoint its committees – probably following a break for lunch.

Much of the work of establishing who sits on which body will have been done at group level beforehand, and the various group leaders will have got together to sort things out, which might well involve a little wheeling and dealing. However, total agreement on all committees is seldom achieved, and there will probably be a vote or two to tidy up the loose ends.

Somewhere in the process, each committee may meet to elect its chair and appoint its sub committees, and also decide on which Members will represent the Council on the various outside bodies. Only if some matter of substance and urgency needs a decision will any other matter be discussed at the Annual Meeting, and such things do happen from time to time. In fact, the whole thing is very different from the usual full council meeting, but does serve to introduce you to the way things are done.

Questions, amendments, 'speaking to'

Annual Meeting apart, the major function of a full council meeting
is to ratify, amend or reject decisions reached by the Council's
committees. It's not the only function; other matters may well be
decided, but perusal of committee minutes is the solid core of the
meeting. You will have received your copy of all the minutes
around two weeks before council, and your group will have met to
decide what line you are to take over the various issues presented.
That's the point at which you decide whether you, personally, wish
to take any action at council, and how you intend to set about it.
Basically, you have three opportunities to put your oar in.

As each set of committee minutes are called by the chairman of
the Council, the chair of that committee rises to present his minutes,
and move that they be accepted by council. Some other committee
member, commonly the vice chair, seconds the motion. The ensuing debate is divided into three sections. First, the council chairman asks for 'questions on the minutes,' and any member may rise
and pose such a question on any matter covered in those minutes.
When all such questions are posed, the committee chair will
endeavour to answer them.

The next stage is for the council chairman to call for 'amendments to the minutes,' and this is the point when most serious debate
takes place. You will then be called upon to vote on each amendment, which if passed becomes part of the minutes under scrutiny.
Finally, when all amendments are dealt with, opportunity is given
to all members to speak on any subject covered by the minutes, but
it's too late to change things. That's been done at amendment stage.

Questions off the minutes

All of that refers to actions already taken by the various committees,
but one way to raise other matters is to pose a 'question off the
minutes' in a period of the council meeting set aside for that
purpose. Having given the appropriate amount of notice – usually
three or four days – and supplying your question in writing, you put
your question to the appropriate committee chairman. If you don't
like the answer you get, the council chairman may have it in his
discretion to allow supplementary questions if he thinks it justified,
but this varies from council to council.

Please note, you can only use this procedure if the subject you
wish to raise is not covered by an item elsewhere on the council's
agenda. It's worth checking beforehand, because you can look, and
feel, a complete idiot if you spend time putting a beautifully

phrased and barbed question, only to have the committee chair say
'Don't worry, that's covered by minute XYZ of the committee
minutes.'

Notices of motion
Questions off the minutes provide an excellent vehicle for asking
for action, or embarrassing the opposition, but there is a more
substantial method of getting decisions made about matters not
covered by committee minutes. It's the **notice of motion** procedure.
In effect, a member may seek to put a motion to full council having
given the appropriate notice in writing. Such motions must be on
the council's agenda, so notices of motion may well have to be in
the chief executive hands a full two weeks before council.

Procedures for dealing with this situation vary widely
throughout the country, but, typically, the Council chairman will
decide at the meeting whether it is more appropriate to deal with
the matter then and there, or refer it to a subsequent committee
meeting and therefore go through the usual process. If that is the
case, members are often given a chance to change council's collec-
tive mind, and vote on whether to debate the matter right away. If
you can cite urgency or overriding public interest in your favour,
you may succeed in doing just that. However, your council may do
things differently, so make some enquiries about it.

In camera
A Council, or more commonly, a committee, may decide that it
should debate some delicate matter with the press and public
excluded. There is a statutory process for this, giving conditions
which must be met before such action can be taken – usually, that
it is not in the public interest for the matter to be discussed in public.
Before such **in camera** decisions may be taken, the motion to
exclude press and public must be put and, if necessary, debated and
carried, with the appropriate section of the Act of Parliament quoted
in the motion.

The press absolutely hate this procedure, and it isn't one to be
embarked upon lightly, but sometimes there isn't much alternative
– as when financial details are to be discussed, the revelation of
which could cost the council a great deal of money.

Getting advice
All of this might seem a little daunting, at first, but once you get
into the swing of things it isn't all that difficult to assimilate. If in

doubt, ask the chief executive, or someone in his department. You'll find officers very helpful in this respect, helping you to frame amendments, questions or notices of motion, if you want them to. Some authorities even have officers whose duties are specifically to assist members in different ways.

COMMITTEES

As you'll have seen, much of the substantive work of the Council is done by the committees, with council itself acting in a 'sweeper' role. It's very nice to be able to wow your colleagues with flights of oratory, impress the press enough to be quoted regularly in the local paper, but you'll really stand or fall as an effective councillor by the role you play in committee. And that's very different from appearing at full council.

Although many standing orders and rules of debate apply as much to committees as they do to council, you'll find that things are much more informal. Whereas it's usually the form to stand when speaking at council, you may discover that you can remain seated at committee, for example. Similarly, although Members are usually only allowed to speak once on any given item at council, and that for a limited time, you may be able to have more than one bite at the cherry at committee, and may not be restricted in the length of your contribution.

Much depends on the chair, who can make things as formal or informal as he likes. Get on well with him, and you can probably do more than if he dislikes you. After all, though he will, no doubt, try to be as fair as he ought to be, he's only human, and it's amazing how some people can fail to catch the chair's eye whenever they want to. If you intend to do something contentious – and you will, sooner or later – it does no harm at all to tip the chair off beforehand. Just how long beforehand, depends on whether he's on your side of the house or not. It's one thing being courteous enough to enable the chair to run the meeting expeditiously, but quite another giving him enough notice of an ambush to prepare his own ammunition.

One of the most common complaints made by committee chairs is that too many things are raised on full council which could quite well be dealt with by committee. There is substance in that contention, and you can often handle a problem by asking the appropriate chair to place the matter on the agenda for the next committee meeting. It also enables you to make your point at least twice – in committee and at full council.

This is equally true if you do not happen to be a member of the committee in question. Most authorities have a system whereby non-members of a committee may attend as an observer, and the chair may, if he feels like it, invite you to speak on the matter you asked him to raise. But obviously, you can't vote.

Amendments

When attending committee, you will have been provided with an agenda, and with the relevant papers for each item. These will have been written by various officers who will also be at the meeting, prepared to defend their reports, and the recommendations made therein. If no one disagrees, then the recommendations become resolutions, and are submitted to full council. If there is a difference of opinion, then any Member may seek to make an amendment. That's when the debate really gets under way, and you'll win some and lose some. Do, however, make sure you have a seconder before you make an amendment, if you possibly can. There's nothing worse than proposing what you conceive to be a brilliant idea, only to have it fail with a dull thud because no one seconds it.

Matters of urgency

The last item on the agenda is usually 'any other business', or very commonly, 'any other urgent business'. Usually, this item is used by the chair and the officers to raise any matter which has cropped up after the agenda was prepared, but you can also ask for a matter to be discussed as a 'matter of urgency'. If the chair agrees, then you can have your discussion. If he doesn't, then the least he can do is place the matter on a future agenda. But don't raise matters on committee which could quite easily be settled by a phone call to an officer. That simply annoys everyone.

DEBATE

Debate is the heart of the whole process of local democracy. The councillor who knows how to debate is the successful one, and much of that ability comes with experience. However, there are things you can do to short circuit the learning process. Notably, you know your rules of debate, back, front and sideways – after all, you have to know the rules before you can bend them with impunity. It's also worth remembering that taking part in a debate isn't like making a speech. You may not have time to prepare, you may be interrupted – you may even find yourself out of order. The golden rule is to do your homework. All that reading may be a chore, but it really is indispensable.

Prepared speeches

If you are making an amendment, or otherwise opening the batting for your group then you will probably know about if beforehand, and will be able to prepare your speech accordingly. Various Councillors have different ways of setting about this, depending to a large extent on their own style and facility with words, but everyone would agree that reading word-for-word from a prepared script does not help to convey the sort of impression you would wish, and should be avoided if at all possible.

Some people think through their speech, and jot down notes in headline form. Others find that it's a good thing to write – or better, type, because you'll want to make a copy available to the press – the whole thing out. They don't do this because they intend to read it out on the day, but because the process structures your speech for you, and also fixes the whole thing firmly in your mind, making it easier for you to make all the points you had intended, even if you are interrupted by points of order or personal explanation.

In theory, speeches are always made to just one person – the chair, and not to the meeting in general; apart from that the structure of a prepared speech to council is the same as any other. And don't forget that there's nothing to stop you using the odd visual aid now and then. Here's an example,

(The Mayor calls upon you to speak)

Introduction	'Thank you Mr Mayor.'
Visual aid	*You flourish a very large and sharp hook.*
The fish hook	'How would you, Mr Mayor, like to have this stuck through your top lip?'
The bridge	'Because that is what is happening, every day, to dozens of our fellow creatures right on the outskirts of our town.'
The body	*You then go on to make an anti-angling speech, and explain why fishing should not be allowed on a stretch of Council-owned water.*

The close   'Mr Mayor, wildlife is important, and we on this
                     Council, should be doing our part in its preser-
                     vation. I very much hope that Council will vote
                     against this Resolution.'

You see the idea? You need a 'fish hook' to grab attention (if you
do use a visual aid of any sort, get it out of the way quickly), a
'bridge' to get you into the body of your speech, and a 'close' to
urge fellow Members to vote your way.

Speaking off the cuff

That structure rapidly becomes second nature, even when you wish
to take part in the cut-and-thrust of debate, and don't have a
thoroughly prepared speech. In those cases, you won't be the first
speaker on the issue in question, so you will have opportunities to
make notes about previous speakers' contributions, and time to
think out the way you will support or refute them. By all means,
add your weight to your colleagues, but try not simply to repeat the
points they have made without adding any new thoughts. Something like, 'I thoroughly agree with Councillor Brown when he says
. . . But I wonder if he's also thought that . . .' is the type of thing
to look for.

This sort of off-the-cuff debate is one of the delights of being a
councillor, and should be very civilised in its tone. There is no need
to descend to abuse or personal comment; indeed such things only
get in the way, and destroy much of the effectiveness of what you
are saying. Above all, *never* lose your cool, however strongly you
may feel about an issue. If you do, you become a sitting duck for
the opposition, and in extreme cases, may be liable to have motions
passed against you, requiring you to stop speaking, or even leave
the meeting.

Finally, the off-the-cuff debate is where having done your homework really pays dividends. It gives you confidence, and you may
well discover errors in the opposition's case.

Hanging your hat

Most of the meetings you attend will be controlled by a fixed
agenda, or by the minutes of previous committee meetings. You
can't raise any issue you want to, unless you can find an item which
may be said to relate to it. But that relationship can be pretty
tenuous, and this provides the basis for that grand old council
institution known as 'hanging your hat'. And it's amazing just

where your headgear can be suspended if you look carefully enough.

Some years ago, a good example arose at a Council meeting in Buckinghamshire. Council was considering the minutes of the Environmental Services Committee at the time, which contained an item about new regulations concerning the storage of petrol containers. It was all completely non-controversial, and no one had any intention of debating the item.

Then one Councillor, a representative of the local Ratepayers Association, rose and said, 'May I call members' attention to item no. 123, relating to petrol containers. An abandoned motor vehicle may contain petrol, and therefore comes under the provisions of these new regulations. May I ask the chairman what he intends to do about the unsightly cars abandoned in various parts of the town, and isn't it time we got to grips with this problem?'

It's amazing what a little ingenuity can do.

Points of order and of personal explanation

A point of order may be raised when a ruling is needed on one of the council's standing orders, which may seem to be in danger of being broken, in the stated opinion of a member. Not that he necessarily does hold that opinion; the cry of 'Point of order' may simply be a ploy to get a comment in. By the time the chairman has ruled that that is not a point of order, the comment has been made. If you're going to use this stratagem, be sure that you know the standing order under which you are operating – just in case you're asked.

Similarly, any member is allowed a point of personal explanation if he considers that a later speaker has misunderstood something he said. It's amazing how many fine shades of meaning can be evinced by members trying to convince people that he never said that at all, and what he really meant was . . .

10
Developing a Public Life

CIVIC RESPONSIBILITIES

Being a councillor doesn't stop at head-to-head confrontations with the opposition in the Council chamber, or in doing your best to help constituents with problems. There are also all the other occasions where you are asked to represent your authority in a variety of ways. Don't underestimate this aspect of the job: it is highly important from the council's point of view, and can be useful public relations as far as you are concerned.

Almost inevitably, you will find yourself appointed to some outside bodies which have Council representation on their management committees. Local community relations councils, law centres, tenants' associations would be typical examples, while sometimes, the council may ask for representation on charitable bodies to which they give an annual grant.

The point here is that you are representing the *Council* and that the authority's policy on any given matter is the one which you should be supporting. It matters not in the least if you believe that policy to be wrong: you must express it and vote accordingly. After all, it's perfectly possible to say, 'This is the Council's policy, with which I don't necessarily agree, but . . .' If you feel you can't do that, then you'd better resign and let someone else do the job.

Local groups

You will also find yourself drafted on to other organisations by virtue of your position as a councillor, rather than being appointed to them by your authority. Community associations within your own ward may want you, local sports clubs may think it a good idea to have your help, especially if they intend to seek grants for one purpose or another, and so on. Or your political affiliation may look for representation on some influential local body.

In these cases, it's up to you how you play it; you're not bound by council policy. Indeed, some such organisations offer you a good platform to oppose that policy. No doubt you'll want to do your fair share of such work, but it's very easy to overdo it, unless you're careful. After all, if you're a lifelong supporter of your local rugby club, then you'll find it difficult to refuse an invitation to join their committee, but you won't do yourself any good if you accept and then find you can't turn up to many meetings. And don't make any mistake about it – sooner or later such organisations are going to want their pound of flesh. They're going to ask you to do something or other for them at Council level. As long as you realise that from the outset . . .

Public meetings

You may be asked to sit on the platform at public meetings, usually held to discuss some contentious issue. You have to do this, but it's a potential minefield, and you will do well to prepare yourself thoroughly before you go. Almost invariably such meetings have a political dimension; your opposition may well be attending in force, and are probably out to *get* you.

Don't let that worry you too much. As a speaker from the platform you have all the advantages: you can dominate proceedings, speak for as long as you like, and use your native wit and charm to demolish critics from a position of strength. But make sure you really know what's going on.

Civic events

If your council has a thriving civic scene, and most do above parish or neighbourhood council level, then you'll be expected to do your bit to support it. This can, on occasion, be enjoyable, interesting, or an outright bore. However, the civic dimension is an important part of the local government scene, and is much valued by the large majority of the public at large. It is also the way to 'sell' your area to visiting notables or groups, and to say 'thanks' to individuals or organisations who have achieved something noteworthy.

This is particularly important where your council chairman is the Mayor, and therefore you have a certain amount of pomp and circumstance. If, for example, the council is processing 'in state' with robes, macebearers, and the rest, perhaps to a cathedral or parish church, it looks very bad if His Worship can only call on a handful of councillors to follow him. What's more, people notice it, and it doesn't reflect well on either the truant councillors, or the council itself. Looking to the future, you have a better chance of attaining civic office yourself if you are a regular supporter of the civic scene.

Civic receptions are also important, although you are much more likely to be regaled with a chipolata on a stick than with smoked salmon and caviar, and council plonk isn't exactly Chateau Lafitte Rothschild. Such events give you opportunities to meet interesting and useful people, which can pay you dividends in the long run. Receptions do tend to be attended by your area's important people, and your own regular presence at them tends to get you numbered among them in popular esteem, which may be a slightly cynical view, but happens to be true.

There is another factor, too. The sense of history evoked by a civic event can be a salutory experience. There you are, dressed in your newly-acquired robe and hat, strolling gently down the main street of your city. As a new councillor, you are at the tail of the procession, with only a few council officers behind you, and the Mayor, macebearers and swordbearer in front of you. People have turned out to watch, and policemen are regulating the route. It's a safe bet that, at some point, you will realise that a great many good people have done this walk before you, and a great many more will do so after you're forgotten. You're merely a link in a chain which may stretch back over the centuries – a custodian, if you like, of a certain set of values which are unique to Britain. You'll probably feel as much humility as pride.

Playing away

There will be occasions when you find yourself representing your council at venues outside your area. This can be close at hand, as when a County Council arranges a meeting with District Councillors within the shire, or it could be a long distance away, perhaps at a local government conference, or on a visit to a twin town. In such cases, the advice would be – grab the opportunity, because you can learn a very great deal about how other Authorities do things, and perhaps they may be better at some things than you are.

Conferences and seminars are particularly interesting: they wouldn't be held unless there was mutual advantage to be gained. If you're attending one of those, you'll almost certainly be accompanied by one or more Members from opposing groups, but in this instance, you're all on the same side, so there should be no problem. You may also have an officer or two along, which gives you an excellent opportunity for a little discreet brain picking, arm twisting or lobbying.

Twin towns
Visits to twin towns are quite different. They are an exercise in inter-European understanding, and valuable in that light, if nothing else. Twin towns are usually selected because they are equivalents to your own area in foreign countries, and when you visit them, the Maire, Oberburgermeister, or whatever, will be seizing the opportunity to sell his town to you like crazy, showing you the sights, impressing you with what his borough has to offer. You'll also be wined and dined to a standard which your own Authority probably can't match. Which can be worrying, because you're probably going to have to invite them on a return visit.

There is a lot of nonsense talked in the press about 'jollies on the Poll Tax' with regards to twin town visits, and it wouldn't be right to say that such events have not been abused occasionally. In fact, the vast majority of authorities treat such matters very responsibly, using the twin town system to foster links between the two towns concerned, at local school and club level as much as at civic level. If you do go on a twin town visit, you'll be expected to pay at least part of your way, and won't get a free trip. A typical arrangement is where the host town provides accommodation and hospitality, but visiting councillors pay their own air fare, and aren't allowed to claim any expenses. If you can afford it, do go. It's well worth it.

TAKING THE CHAIR

Unless your elections have thrown up a real night of the long knives, it's unlikely that you will be offered a chair in your first term of office. However, you're going to have to function at meetings controlled by chairpersons, so it will help you to understand a little about how the system operates. Furthermore, it isn't nearly so uncommon for new members to become vice chairs: some organisations consider this to be a good way to gain experience quickly. There will also be the occasions when special working parties are set up to consider one-off issues, and if you happen to have special experience or expertise relevant to the problem, then you could find yourself in the hot seat, so to speak.

The first thing to realise is that the chair of a programme committee has a great deal of power, not all of it obvious. He, or she, can make life very difficult for you as an 'ordinary' Member, or can be very helpful. Politics and personalities being what they are, it isn't wise to assume that a member of your group will be helpful, or that an opposition chair will be obstructive: there may, for example, be important implications for a chairman's own ward in what you are trying to achieve.

A chairman has the everyday ear of the important officers. If a chief officer knows his own chair is keen on something, then it tends to get done. Second, the chair has a great deal of control over what finds its way on to the committee agenda and what doesn't. He will see reports from officers before you do, and can get them altered if he doesn't like them. At the meeting itself, he won't block your right to speak, but he does decide the order in which speakers are called, which can be a powerful weapon in the hands of an experienced operator.

What all this means is that you're not just dealing with the person sitting at the head of the table. You're up against a system. If you realise that, you have a better chance of coping with it.

The art of chairing

Chairing is a minor art in its own right, and it would be quite possible to write a book this size solely on that subject. Some chairpersons are born for the job, some are manufactured, and some people will never make a decent chairman as long as they have a hole in their nose. It's no job for the indecisive, or even for the excessively kindhearted, because sometimes you have to be cruel to your personal and political friends. You need to be forthright, clear thinking, well-informed and even a little clinical in your approach. A streak of deviousness is a distinct advantage, and it doesn't do any harm to have a sense of humour.

When you are in the chair of a Council committee, you are the boss. You may defer to your Mayor or your group leader at all other times, but if they happen to sit on your committee, then they must expect your word to be law. And they don't always like that fact.

You must know the procedure inside out, and be very aware of the powers of your committee – whether decisions must be referred to full council, or whether some may, or should, be taken under delegated powers conferred on the committee by government or council.

Although committee meetings tend to be less formal than full council ones, there is a level of formality which must be observed for a variety of reasons, not least that you can get through business more expeditiously that way. Indeed, many experienced chairmen contend that the more formal a meeting the better. For example, the practice of always speaking through the chair doesn't just prevent chaos and unseemly wrangles, it also preserves personal relationships. You can have a severe disagreement with a fellow member through the chair without offending him, but a hammer-and-tongs across the table can cost you a friend.

The level of formality is never more important than when taking a vote. Never let anything go through 'on the nod' because it could be challenged later. If a vote looks like being unanimous, you should still go through the motions. Simply ask, 'Anyone against?' and allow time for members to put their hands up.

Dealing with amendments

Amendments can be particularly tricky for an inexperienced chair, because you may have more than one to the same resolution. The traditional procedure, however, takes you through the process logically, and there should be no problem so long as you adhere to it. As follows:

1. You are debating a report, and someone **moves** that the recommendations made therein be adopted. The motion is duly seconded. It therefore becomes a **resolution**.
2. Someone else raises an **amendment**, again duly seconded.
3. A third Member makes another amendment and also finds a seconder.
4. A fourth Member, complete with seconder, tables a third amendment.

- Your first action is to put the first amendment to the meeting. It falls, so no further action need be taken.

- You then put the second amendment. That is passed by the meeting. It then becomes the **substantive motion**, and you put it to the meeting again, which is normally a formality. In effect, it now has the same status as the original resolution.

- You then put the third amendment. If it falls, that is the end of the matter. If it passes, then it must be put again as the substantive motion, and then becomes the resolution which will be presented to full council.

It sounds complicated, but it isn't really, just as long as you work your way steadily through the accepted procedure.

Voting from the chair

Don't forget that as chairman, you have, in effect, two votes. You may vote when a question is first put, and if the count is equal you have a casting vote, which can be useful, but can also put you well and truly on the spot. Although the tradition is that a casting vote is used to preserve the status quo, that's a convention honoured at least as much in the breach as the observance, and if the issue has a political dimension, the pressure upon the chair to vote one way or another can be intense.

If the issue happens to be in the form of an amendment there is sometimes an escape clause you can use; amendments to resolutions have to be passed. If votes are equal, then they fall, and the resolutions stand. You don't have to use your casting vote.

In all these matters, and others like them, you will have your chief officer sitting alongside you, and a member of the chief executive's department on the other side. They will guide you through any minefield, but you may not always wish to take their advice, and a thorough knowledge of procedure may enable you to take a contrary view.

The chair's relationships with council officers

This brings us to relationships which a good chairman has with the officers of his or her department. The last thing they should be is confrontational, even when you believe there to be a great deal wrong with the department, and have every intention to put things right. If you simply can't get on with your chief officer, then one of you will have to go, and you can't assume it's going to be the officer. If you think you'll have problems of this sort, it's better for all concerned if you don't accept the chair in the first place.

One very experienced West Country chairman tenders this advice:

'At the start of each civic year, as soon as possible after the Annual Meeting, I get together with my chief officer and his section heads. I spend an hour or so reviewing the situation with each of them, finding out the problems which are currently worrying them most, and inviting ideas. I also encourage them to express any thoughts they have about new initiatives. The chief officer's secretary takes notes and later sends me an aide memoire.

'That done, I make virtually the same speech each year, and make no apology for doing so. In effect, it goes, 'Look – the man who never made a mistake never made anything. You're going to put your foot in it, on occasion. When you do, tell me about it, and don't try to flannel me. You won't get away with it, anyway. If you do that, then I'll back you to the hilt, and defend you to the rest of the world to the best of my ability. Of course, what I might do to you behind closed doors is another matter.

'The reverse side of that coin is that I am just as likely to make a mistake as anyone else, and when I do so, I shall expect the same sort of support from you. Right. The meeting is now closed, and I intend to trot down to the pub for a quiet drink. If anyone likes to join me, they're very welcome.'

That's one way to get off on the right foot. It establishes friendly and supportive relations, while leaving no one in any doubt about who's boss. It might not be exactly your style, but you see the technique; it's one that can be adapted for your own use.

Many chairs set up a regular weekly meeting with their chief officers, just to keep abreast with things. That's all right as far as it goes, but it isn't as effective as the frequent visit unannounced. Any time you're in your civic offices, make a point of visiting the department. You don't need a reason – just turn up. When you do that, it's a good idea to make the chief officer's office your final port of call: make a point of sticking your head around a few doors and simply saying 'good morning'. One thing you must simply not allow is for your chief officer to insulate you from the rest of the department, and therefore act as a filter, only letting you know what he wishes you to know. Of course, a lot depends on personalities, but methods such as these can pay big dividends, and keep the Department firmly on your side because that's where they want to be, rather than have to be.

The pre meeting

It's unwise for a chair to turn up 'cold' to a meeting of the committee, knowing little more than the average committee member. Most councils have a Pre Meeting system which allows the chair to be briefed, and the officers to know the likely turn of events. The form of the pre meeting varies widely, ranging from an informal briefing session between chair and chief officer, with other officers on hand if needed, to a thoroughly formal meeting with officers of other interested departments, the vice chairman, and representatives of opposition groups present, too. It's normally at the discretion of the chair what form the pre meeting takes, but some system is essential.

There's little point in holding such a meeting on the day before committee: you may need time to receive additional reports, to rearrange the order in which the agenda will be taken, to consult with member colleagues, or any number of other purposes. You may also wish to do additional homework yourself.

TAKING CIVIC OFFICE

At the time you stand for Council, it will never have crossed your mind that you might one day be Mayor of your town or city – if it's fortunate enough to have one, that is. But suddenly, there he or she is, presiding over meetings which you are summoned to attend, and the whole thing becomes a real prospect. And so it should; civic office is the highest honour to which a local councillor may aspire. County Councils, of course, just have chairmen, but much of what can be said about Mayors can be applied to them, and it's worth concluding with a brief description of what duties and privileges civic officers have in the 1990s.

To some extent, the civic scene changed with local government reorganisation in 1973/4. At that time, towns and cities were given the option of retaining the privileges they had always had. If they wished to, then they had to apply to the crown, which, by the royal prerogative, granted charters to reinstate the offices of Mayors and Sheriffs. Most ancient boroughs availed themselves of this, and many towns who hadn't had a Mayor before then were also granted the privilege.

In fact, there were always pecking orders among Mayors. Large towns, and some smaller ones, have Lord Mayors. Then, in descending order, we have Right Worshipful Mayors, Worshipful Mayors, and plain straightforward Mayors. The distinction doesn't make any difference, nowadays, but boroughs tend to cling to their ancient rights and privileges, and why shouldn't they?

Sheriffs

All County Councils have Sheriffs, but less than two dozen towns and cities do, nowadays, which is a shame, because the office is, in most cases, older than that of Mayor, stretching back to the Saxon 'shire reeve'. Today, the Sheriff's office is almost purely civic, although some authorities have protected it by combining the office of Sheriff with that of vice chairman of the council.

Indeed, the calls on the Mayor's time seem to be ever increasing, and the Sheriff can take a great deal of the load from the first citizen's shoulders.

For example, in the old days, a Mayor wouldn't have anything to do with anything as crass as 'trade', but these days, helping to promote the industrial and commercial life of the area is emphatically part of the Mayor's job. This has increased the workload, and it's good to have a Sheriff to take over if the Mayor is in danger of becoming double booked. A mere 'vice chairman' doesn't have quite the same ring to it.

How are Mayors elected?

To be strictly accurate, they aren't. The technical position is that the Mayor is appointed under royal charter. However, ever since 1973, the Mayor, as Chairman of Council, has to be an elected Member of the authority, and can't be appointed from outside, so an election of some sort is inevitable. Mayor-making ceremonies involve a resolution along the lines of 'so-and-so is elected and hereby appointed Mayor of Strawbury-on-Sea for the ensuing year.'

How the choice is arrived at varies widely. In some areas, there is an element of seniority in the selection. This does prevent unseemly political wrangles, but can generate in-fighting, because several qualifying councillors may well have arrived on council at the same time. In other boroughs, the Deputy Mayor automatically steps up to the higher office. Commonly, however, it all comes down to a straightforward vote of the council. If one group has overall control, they tend to take the civics as well, because that gives them the Mayor's casting vote. In 'hung' councils, the wheeling and dealing can be horrendous, but often, the various groups take it in turns. You'll soon find out how it works in your authority. You'll probably be lobbied unmercifully about it from day one.

Mayoral duties at civic events

The sheer variety of events to which the Mayor is invited is overwhelming. Most find they attend over 1,000 of them in the civic year. And it usually is just one year, whereas chairmen of county and district councils tend to remain in office for longer, sometimes much longer, periods. As Mayor, you could easily find yourself attending a royal garden party on one day, and presenting a local pub's darts cups the day after. You could be in full robes with macebearers and swordbearer in the morning, in light summery clothes at a garden fête in the afternoon, and attending a ball or banquet in full evening dress in the evening.

The trick is to be completely natural. Don't try to be anything you aren't, because there is always someone around who knew you 'way back when', and anyway, you can't keep it up for twelve solid months. Any Mayor rapidly develops a split personality. If you're kicking off a football match, for example, the crowd will probably erupt into cheers as you walk out on the field. But you soon realise that it isn't you they're cheering – it's the chain, 'their' Mayor, representing the fans themselves, someone with whom they can identify.

Inevitably, some events are more enjoyable than others, but a good Mayor doesn't allow himself the privilege of picking and choosing. The safe rule is to accept the first invitation you receive for a given time and day, and stick to it, although it can be extremely galling to have agreed to attend a (to you) dry as dust meeting, only to have to turn down a later invitation to something you'd really enjoy. There are exceptions of course: a royal visit, for example, takes precedence over everything, and if a sudden Special Council Meeting is called for any reason, then all your social engagements for that time go by the board.

It's quite possible, especially on a summer Saturday, to attend seven or eight engagements in one day, but most Mayors find that they do not operate as efficiently during the last few events of such a day as they do at the beginning, so it's as well to confine yourself to three or four.

Demands on time and money

As you'll gather, civic office takes *time* – a great deal of it. Many Mayors and Sheriffs have done superb jobs while also working at a 'nine-to-five' job, but it is difficult, and you to have to have a very understanding employer. The law provides that employers must allow 'reasonable time' for any councillor to fulfill his or her office, but the demands of the mayoralty are a little extreme, and it's as well to consult before deciding whether to take it on. On the other hand, many employers welcome the fact that they have the Mayor on the strength, and may see some commercial advantage in it.

The other thing the mayoralty demands is money. Although the Mayor will receive an allowance to help him perform the office, it never pays all the bills. Ladies need clothes, you may have to buy a morning suit, the Mayor's drinks cabinet can seem to be a bottomless pit. There are also the 'unconsidered trifles'; the Mayor buys more raffle tickets than anyone else, for example, (which also means he probably wins more prizes, which can be embarrassing) and you'll find yourself putting a fiver into the collection plate on Sundays. It's as well to be aware of this, but you can't expect to experience such a marvellous year without paying *something* for it.

The business end

Everyone forgets that there's a 'business' side to the job, and that it's as important as the social dimension. Indeed, there may be occasions in the year when the Mayor *is* the council, having to make important decisions quickly, hoping that council will ratify them later. And of course, the Mayor is chairman of the council.

In essence, chairing a full council meeting is no different than chairing a committee, with its procedure and rules of debate, plus the readily-available advice of professional officers at all times. However, pressures are greater simply because the meeting is larger, and probably longer. There is also the fact that members attending the meeting include past civics and past and present chairmen, at least some of whom may be out to *get* you. When chairing council, the Mayor can't afford to relax for a minute. Whereas members may be able to nip out of the meeting for a breather or a smoke, now and then, the chairman can't.

A good-humoured attitude to this is essential. It's quite possible, even desirable, to adhere to the letter of the standing orders, while keeping things perfectly pleasant. The advice would be to start your year in the chair perhaps a little tougher than you mean to go on. If you have the council whipped into shape, it's easy to back off a little later in the year, but the converse isn't true. You can't start off indulgently, and then expect to stiffen up later.

Of course, there are more ways of skinning a cat. One Mayor of Gloucester found himself chairing an extremely important debate in his very first full council of the civic year. So contentious was the issue that council passed a resolution to suspend standing orders so that Members could speak for more than the normal five minutes. Council also had a 'no smoking' policy at meetings, and the Mayor rapidly discovered that one or two members had lit up cigarettes.

Now that particular Mayor was a smoker himself, and if he couldn't have a fag, no one else was going to either, so he asked members to extinguish the offending items. 'But, Mr Mayor,' objected one smoker, 'You've suspended standing orders!' The Mayor pointed out that the no-smoking policy wasn't a standing order, but a resolution of council, a fact which the offending member knew perfectly well. The whole thing was a try-on, a way to test the new chairman. The Mayor had the last laugh, though. He didn't let council go to tea until 6.45pm.

Mayoral gender

It may be objected that the Mayor has always been described as 'he' in this chapter. The fact is that, technically, that is correct. The form of address is always 'Mr Mayor' whether the incumbent is male or female. A Mayoress isn't a lady Mayor, it's a male Mayor's wife or partner.

Things get difficult if one has a lady Mayor with a male partner, who can hardly be called a Mayoress. Usually, this is overcome by simply referring to the consort by his name.

A Sheriff's consort, if female, is commonly called 'Sheriff's Lady', and again, if male simply by his name. In fact there are other words, now, sadly, fallen into disuse. While there's no more honourable or respectful title in the English language than 'Lady', the word 'Shireen' or 'Sheriffeen' does have a certain ring to it.

Local political life is still rather male-orientated and chauvinistic, and in a field so steeped in tradition as civic office, it's not very easy to change it.

However, various formulae have been used in some parts of the country to satisfy everyone, with varying degrees of success. If you feel strongly about it, there's nothing to stop you devising your own.

The greatest experience of all

The winning of civic office may be very far from your thoughts at this moment, and you may even feel that it's something you do not aspire to, and won't ever be interested in. But it is the greatest experience local government has to offer, one which not everyone experiences, and which results in a small but secure niche in history. No matter how well you think you know your town, you'll learn a great deal more about it during a civic year, and find out things about people you never knew before.

You will meet people you never thought you would, perhaps even the Queen herself. Important people visiting your town from all over the world will probably pay their respects to the Mayor, and will be entertained by him. You will make contacts and friends who will remain with you for a lifetime. You may even write a book about it.

But there's a long way to go yet. Now go out and fight that first election. And the very best of luck to you, whoever and wherever you are.

Appendix A
What Happens Next in
Local Government?

As this book goes to press, the government's latest Local Government Bill is making its progress through the House of Lords. No one can be certain of the final outcome, but one thing's for sure – the whole pattern of how we organise our local communities and services will be disrupted for the second time in twenty years. Things will never be the same again.

This has enormous implications for a councillor elected in 1992, or the two or three years thereafter. Almost inevitably, there will be periods of confusion while central government tries to sort out the implications of what it has done. Great efforts will be made to minimise this, of course, but the whole subject is so complex that some aspects are bound to slip through the net until, that is, local councils have to administer the new structures, when anomalies will appear. Those of us who were around the last time round will remember the transition period of 1973/4 with feeling.

It adds up to a tremendous and fascinating challenge for the new councillor. There has seldom been a better time to seek election if you relish the thought of being in at the beginning of something new and important, and of influencing the way your town, city or rural community is run. Indeed, it wouldn't be overstating the matter to say that the lives of everyone you know locally will be influenced by the decisions you make in your first term as a local councillor.

Everything is in a state of flux, but some intelligent guesses can be made from what we know of the government's intentions already.

Back to 1972?
The Local Government Act of 1971 provides an excellent example of the intransigence of people faced with the imposition of change they didn't want. People didn't like the boundaries of counties in which they had been born and brought up altered in the cause of an

efficiency which, in too many cases, didn't materialise. Some counties (Rutland, for example) disappeared completely.

Others, such as Avon, were created whether the inhabitants wanted it or not. And there were the uneasy amalgamation of old administrative areas, sometimes forcing traditional rivals to climb into bed with each other.

In many cases, the reaction was simply to ignore the new order of things. That bastion of tradition, the cricketing community, provides an excellent example. If the Test and County Cricket Board had colluded with the new county boundaries, then Middlesex CCC would have ceased to exist, and Lord's would have become an industrial estate. Ian Botham plays for Worcestershire, rather than Hereford and Worcester. Since 1973, Gloucestershire CCC actually has its headquarters in the County of Avon!

Even some individuals managed to pretend that nothing had happened. The late Duke of Beaufort, Master of the Queen's Horse had 'Badminton House, Gloucestershire' rather than 'Badminton House, Avon' on his letterhead until the day he died. The whole situation is an affirmation that government in Great Britain must be by consent rather than imposition.

That's not to say that the 1973 reorganisation was all bad. There are areas where new county boundaries have worked well and will probably not be changed again. However, it seems likely that the *status quo ante* will be re-established in many parts of Britain. You could even end up serving on a different council to the one you originally sought election for!

Back to the Districts

Perhaps the most unpopular change was the one which took powers and responsibilities from the old local councils operating at what are now called district level and gave them to the new county councils. The idea was that 'big is beautiful', and that economies of scale would result. In the event, that wasn't always the case, but it was the increasing sense of remoteness which has always offended many electors. If, for example, you had a problem with your child's education, then you used to be able to trot along to your own town hall and sort things out. After reorganisation, you could well find that the Education Department was based in another town completely, quite a few miles away.

This remoteness has implications at councillor level. Most wards have three district councillors, and the chances are that almost every elector knows at least one of them personally. However, there is only one county councillor for that same ward, and no matter how hard he works, he can't possibly know everyone. For the average resident, therefore, problems of Education or Social Services are much more difficult to solve quickly than getting dustbins emptied or holes in the road mended.

The intention now seems to be to solve the problems of remoteness. It could well be that, in many parts of the country, services will be administered at a more local level, perhaps approximating to the system which obtained before the last Local Government Act. Not surprisingly, the districts tend to be all for this, and intend to fight for it. Indeed, there is already a consortium of around a dozen historic cities who have got together and appointed a firm of parliamentary consultants to represent their interests while the whole legislative process goes on.

But this devolutionary process is probably not appropriate everywhere. The problems of a compact urban area are very different from those of a widespread rural one, and services in the latter case may well be better administered at County level. We shall probably not end up with a homogenous system which is the same wherever you live. In some cases, your input as a councillor elected while the new process of change is going on could be vital. How do you feel about your own local area? Where should it go from here?

A regional dimension?

The intention appears to be to go for a unitary system. To establish a situation where, ignoring parish and neighbourhood councils, which will still have a role to play, services are administered by one authority, be it at county or district level. Unfortunately, there *are* services which don't sit happily in such an arrangement. The police provide an excellent example.

Police forces, in the main, are still organised under the old county constabulary system, with some exceptions such as the Metropolitan Police and the Thames Valley Police. Each force has its own Chief Constable, and is administered by a – frequently uneasy – partnership of County Police Committee and Home Office. It's obvious that police forces can't proliferate by making them responsible to their local district council. Indeed, there is a feeling in some quarters that we should have one, monolithic national police force.

At least two of the three major political parties appear to be committed to some form of regional government, with democratic involvement. We could see something of the sort emerging from the new legislation. If so, and if central government, of whatever political colour or even a mixture, goes according to form, then such regional bodies will not be directly elected. In many parts of the country there is at least one election every year as it is, and few people would want another one. It seems probable that any new regional body would consist of members appointed by government, and some by local authorities. But you never know.

The challenge

What all this means is that councillors elected in the early to mid-1990s are marching into the unknown. From that point of view it's an excellent period to get yourself elected, because there has seldom been a better time to make a name for yourself.

Furthermore, if the experience of the last reorganisation is any guide, there will be more seats up for grabs as the new system works itself out. There will be those experienced councillors who were probably thinking of retiring anyway, and who will find that transition period a good time to do so. There will also be those who don't like the new system and will lose interest. On the other hand, there may be more people eager to seek election: those who had no interest at all in serving on a remote authority, but will jump at the chance of representing the old home town.

People cutting their teeth for the first time now are to be envied. Just so long as you know what you're getting yourself into.

Appendix B
Campaign Notebook

Diary	*Date*
Local selection committee meeting	. . . .
Central selection committee meeting	. . . .
Ward committee meetings	. . . .
	. . . .
	. . . .
	. . . .
Nomination papers received	. . . .
Nomination papers back to Agent	. . . .
Canvass starts	. . . .
Literature received	. . . .
Literature delivered by	. . . .
Posters received	. . . .
Posters erected by	. . . .
Counting Agents, guests appointed by	. . . .
ELECTION DAY	. . . .

Telephone Directory   *Number*

Ward Chairman (Home)   . . . .

                (Bus.)   . . . .

Ward Secretary (Home)   . . . .

                (Bus.)   . . . .

Campaign Manager (Home)   . . . .

                (Bus.)   . . . .

Agent (Home)   . . . .

      (Bus.)   . . . .

Central office   . . . .

Electoral Registration Officer   . . . .

Returning Officer   . . . .

Committee Rooms   . . . .

Others   . . . .

                                    . . . .

                                    . . . .

                                    . . . .

                                    . . . .

                                    . . . .

Glossary

Absent Voters. Electors whose names appear on the Electoral Register, but who do not vote in person. They may have proxy votes or postal votes for a variety of reasons, including health, reasonable absence on Election Day, or be service men or women, for example.

Agenda. Strictly, the list of items to be discussed at a meeting, but the term is sometimes extended to include the whole package of papers – reports, budgets, correspondence etc – which accompanies that list.

Agent. An official, sometimes paid, who is responsible for the conduct and organisation of a political organisation's election campaign in the whole of its local area, rather than in just one Ward. Not to be confused with a Campaign Director or Manager whose responsibilities are for one Ward only.

Annual Meeting. The statutory meeting of a Local Authority at the beginning of each civic year for the purpose of electing Civic Officers, Chairs and Members of Committees, Sub Committees etc, as well as appointing Members to sit on outside bodies.

Assenter. One of eight electors who sign a Candidate's Nomination Paper in addition to the Proposer and Seconder.

Budget. The detailed statement of a Local Authority's income and expenditure intentions for a given civic year.

Campaign Manager/Director. A person appointed by a local Ward organisation to organise its campaign in a single Ward. May be the Candidate himself or herself.

Canvass. The practice of calling on electors to try to ascertain their voting intentions. Hence 'canvassing' and 'canvassers'.

Census. An official count of inhabitants, taken every 10 years, and statistics relating to it.

Chair. More and more often used to describe the elected Member who conducts the affairs of a specific Committee or Sub Committee. The intention is to replace the term 'Chairman', which some see as chauvinistic, and avoid the clumsy 'Chairperson' or

'Chairwoman'. Not universally popular: one long-serving Chairman, on being called 'Chair' for the first time, commented, 'Sir, a chair is something wooden and frequently sat on. I have no intention of being either.'

Consent to Nomination Form. A statutory document required to be signed by a Candidate before standing for election.

Constituency. A division of an area for voting purposes. It is represented in Parliament by an MP.

Constitution. A set of rules for governing an organisation.

Count. The process of counting the votes cast at an election.

Counting Agent. A person, appointed by a Candidate, to look after his or her interests at a Count.

Delegated Powers. Powers delegated by Council to Committees or Officers. Actions taken under delegated powers will be reported to full Council, but not debated, although they may well attract comment.

Dies Non. Days falling within an election period, but not deemed to be part of that period. They include Saturdays, Sundays, Bank Holidays and Good Friday.

Dispensation. Conferred by the Secretary of State for the Environment, allowing a member to speak and/or vote on a matter in which he has a financial or personal interest.

Election Address. A piece of literature supplied by a Candidate to the Electorate. Contains biographical notes, policies, intentions and a personal letter from the Candidate.

Electoral Registration Officer. A full-time official of a Council, responsible for the compilation and maintenance of the Electoral Roll, as well as assisting Candidates at Election time, checking nomination papers, etc.

Electoral Returning Officer. A Council official, frequently the Authority's Chief Executive Officer, or Solicitor, responsible for the conduct of an election. Officiates at the Count, assisted by Deputies for each Ward, and is the final judge on matters of disagreement.

Group. A grouping, usually political, of elected Members within a Council who have common aims and ideologies.

Imprint. The statement indicating the printer and publisher of any piece of election literature. This is a statutory requirement, and must appear on every copy of any such literature.

Independents. Members who hold no allegiance to a political party or other organised body. They may well, however, be members of a Council Group.

Interest. Financial or personal interests held by a Member in a given topic must, by law, be declared at any meeting where that topic is discussed. The Member cannot then speak or vote (unless he or she has secured a Dispensation; see above), and should leave the meeting for the duration of the appropriate topic.

Interests may sometimes be indirect, as when they are held by a close family member rather than the Councillor. The safe rule is – when in doubt, declare an interest.

'Intro Card'. Short for 'Introduction Card': a piece of literature giving information about a Candidate, handed out to electors during canvassing. May also double as a window bill.

'Knocking Up'. The practice of calling on known pledges on Election Day to persuade them to turn out and vote.

Last Minute Leaflet. A brief piece of literature distributed on the evening of the Election.

Leader. The Leader of the Council is the Member who speaks and acts for the controlling Group, and therefore for the Council itself, on occasion. Where no overall control exists, the Group Leaders co-operate to perform this function. In theory, anyway.

Member. Councillors refer to each other as 'Members'. On occasion, Officers prefer the term too.

Minutes. The record of business of a Council or its constituent bodies. The major function of full Council is to ratify or amend the Minutes of Committees.

Motion. A formal proposal, requiring a decision, put before a meeting.

Nomination Day. The date by which all Candidates must be validly nominated, and after which no further nominations are permissible.

Nomination Paper. Every Candidate is required to produce at least one nomination paper bearing the signatures of a Proposer, a Seconder, and eight Assenters. All such signatories must be registered electors of the Ward in question.

Notice of Election. The notice which appears outside polling stations announcing that an election is to be held on such-and-such a date. It is replaced by the Notice of Poll.

Notice of Poll. States the names of validly-nominated Candidates, with the names of their Nominators.

Notice of Motion. A device by which a Member may raise a matter on full Council which is not covered by any other item on the Agenda.

Officer. Strictly, any employee of a Council, but frequently applied only to 'white collar' workers.

'Outs'. Electors who aren't at home (or don't answer the door) when a canvasser calls.

Petition. A written request to authority signed by many people.

Pledge. An elector who has indicated his support of a particular Candidate.

Point of Order. Raised at any time in a debate by any Member who believes, or purports to believe, that Standing Orders are in danger of being infringed.

Point of Personal Explanation. Any Member may raise a Point of Personal Explanation if he believes, or purports to believe, that a later speaker has misunderstood him.

Postering. The process of erecting posters on prearranged sites.

Press Release. Written statement to the press.

'Pushing Out'. The distribution of election literature.

Quorum. Minimum number of people who must be present at a meeting before any business can be conducted.

Recount. The process of counting votes again, at the demand of a Candidate, when votes cast at a Ward election are close enough to warrant it. They rarely come singly.

Register/Roll. Alternative terms for the list of electors registered to vote at the election.

Rules of Debate. That section of Standing Orders which regulates the conduct of debate.

Standing Orders. The rules laid down by Council, and periodically amended, by which it conducts its affairs.

Surgery. The occasion when a Councillor attends at a pre-arranged time and place to hear complaints, comments and problems of constituents.

Telling. The practice of asking electors to give their register numbers when leaving the Polling Station.

Ward. An electoral district within a Local Authority area.

Whip. An instruction given by a Group meeting which compels Members to vote in an agreed way. Much rarer than the media would have you believe.

Further Reading

Arthur Young Councillor's Handbook: A Practical Guide to Success in Local Government (Harrap/Arthur Young, 1987).

Bird, Polly, *How to Run a Local Campaign* (How To Books, 1989).

Butcher, Hugh, *Local Government and Thatcherism* (Routledge, 1990).

Byrne, A., *Local Government in Britain: Everyone's Guide to How It All Works* (Penguin, 4th edition, 1986).

Chandler, J.A., *Local Government Today* (Manchester University Press, 1991).

Fowler, Alan, *Personnel Policy: The Agenda for Councillors* (Local Government Training Board, 1989).

Hampton, William, *Local Government and Urban Politics* (Longman, 1987).

Hollis, Patricia, *Ladies Elect: Women in English Local Government 1914-1965* (Oxford Clarendon Press, 1987).

Hutt, Jane, *Opening the Town Hall Door: An Introduction to Local Government Politics* (Bedford Square Press, revised edition 1988).

Kingdom, John, *Local Government and Politics in Britain* (Philip Allan, 1991).

Knowles, Raymond, *The Law and Practice of Local Authority Meetings* (ICSA Publishing, 1987).

Longman Directory of Local Authorities (Longman, 1989).

Mellors, Colin & Copperthwaite, Nigel, *Local Government in the Community* (ICSA Publishing, 1987).

Prophet, John, *The Councillor: A Handy Guide to the Functions of Councillors* (Shaw, 1987, 10th edition).

Sheldrake, John, *Municipal Socialism* (Avebury, 1989).

Stewart, John, & Stoker, Gerry, *The Future of Local Government* (Macmillan, 1989).

Young, Ken, *New Directions for County Government* (Association of County Councils, 1989).

Young, Ken, *Professionalism in Local Government: Change and Challenge* (Longman, 1990).

Useful Addresses

Association of Councillors, Town Hall, Ramsden Street, Huddersfield HD1 2TA. Tel: (0484) 22133 ext 209. Founded in 1959, its membership includes about 3,500 individuals and 70 organisations in local government. It is affiliated to the International Union of Local Authorities and the Council of European Municipalities. It publishes the periodical *The Councillor* and a *Bulletin.*

Association of County Councils, 66a Eaton Square, London SW1W 9BH. Tel: (071) 235 1200. Represents non-metropolitan county councils in England and Wales. Publishes the *County Councils Gazette* each month.

Association of District Councils, 9 Buckingham Gate, London SW1E 6LE. Tel: (071) 828 7931. Represents more than 300 non metropolitan district councils in England and Wales and publishes a monthly newsletter and the *District Councils Review.*

Chartered Institute of Public Finance and Accountancy, 3 Robert Street, London WC2N 6BH. Tel: (071) 930 3456. The leading professional body concerned with accountancy and finance matters in local government. Its membership is some 10,000 individuals in the UK and abroad. It publishes the quarterly journal *Public Money* and weekly *Public Finance and Accountancy.* Strong on research and statistical information.

Conservative & Unionist Party, 32 Smith Square, London SW1P 3HH. Tel: (071) 222 9000.

Directory of Social Change, 9 Mansfield Place, London NW3.

The Ecology Party, 36-38 Clapham Road, London SW9. Tel: (071) 735 2485.

The Green Party, 10 Station Parade, Balham High Road, London SW12. Tel: (071) 673 0045.

House of Commons, Westminster, London SW1A 0AA. Tel: (071) 219 3000.

The Institute of Chartered Accountants in England & Wales

(ICAEW), PO Box 433, Chartered Accountants Hall, Moorgate Place, London EC2P 2BJ. Tel: (071) 628 7060.

The Labour Party, 150 Walworth Road, London SE17 1JT. Tel: (071) 703 0833.

Law Centres Federation, Duchess House, 18-19 Warren Street, London W1P 5DB. Tel: (071) 387 8570.

Local Government Reform Society, 14 Princes Avenue, Bognor Regis, West Sussex PO21 2DY. Tel: (0243) 863726. Honorary Secretary Paul Smith. Has a membership of some 1,500 individuals and organisations both in the UK and overseas. Campaigns for more open conduct of local government.

National Association of Citizens' Advice Bureaux, Myddleton House, 115/123 Pentonville Road, London N1 9LZ. Tel: (071) 833 2181.

National Association of Local Councils, 108 Great Russell Street, London WC1B 3LD. Tel: (071) 637 1865. Established in 1947, its membership consists of some 7,500 parish, community and town councils. It publishes the quarterly *Local Council Review* and a number of handbooks.

National Council for Civil Liberties, 21 Tabard Street, London SE1 4LA. Tel: (071) 403 3888.

National Council for Voluntary Organisations, 26 Bedford Square, London WC1B 3HU. Tel: (071) 636 4066. A very large number of bodies are affiliated to the NCVO.

National Federation of Community Organisations, 8-9 Upper Street, London N1 0PQ. Tel: (071) 226 0189.

Plaid Cymru, 51 Cathedral Road, Cardiff CF1 9HD. Tel: (0222) 31944.

Royal Institute of Public Administration, 3 Birdcage Walk, London SW1H 9JH. Tel: (071) 222 2248. Publishes the quarterly journal *Public Administration*.

Scottish Council for Voluntary Organisations, 18-19 Claremont Crescent, Edinburgh EH7 4QD. Tel: (031) 556 3882.

Scottish National Party, 6 North Charlotte Street, Edinburgh EH2 4JH. Tel: (031) 226 3661.

Social & Liberal Democrats, 4 Cowley Street, London SW1P 3NB. Tel: (071) 222 7999.

Trades Union Congress (TUC), Congress House, Great Russell Street, London WC1B 3LS. Tel: (071) 636 4030.

Wales Council for Voluntary Action, Llys Ifor, Crescent Road, Caeffili CF8 1XL. Tel: 869224/8699111.

Index

How to Be an Effective School Governor
Polly Bird

This new book has been written for all those interested in helping to govern their local schools, following the recent educational reforms and advent of local management of schools. Assuming little or no prior knowledge it sets out all the basics from discussing whether to get involved, getting nominated and elected, attending first meetings, taking part in meetings and decision-making, whether on staffing, the school budget, the curriculum, resource planning and other important topics. The book includes a clear statement of the rights and responsibilities of governors under the law, with the aim of helping every individual, whatever their background, to play a full part in shaping the future of the school. Well-signposted with quick-reference headings, the book is complete with helpful checklists, examples, specimen documents, glossary, guide to contacts and further reading, and index. Polly Bird is a graduate of Cambridge University, and qualified teacher, and a firm believer in helping individuals and communities to stand up for their rights.

176pp illus. 0 7463 0553 2. 1991.

How to Run a Local Campaign
Polly Bird

As people battle against vested interests for a better life, this book explains in a clear easy-to-read format the right approach to starting and winning a public campaign. Polly Bird, herself an experienced local campaigner, provides tips, advice and checklists from first steps and publicity through to funds, self-help option, and what to do on completion of a project. Including valuable campaigning address lists, this book is a must for everyone with a cause to fight. 'An excellent beginner's guide to successful campaigning.' *Green Magazine.* 'Contains everything the local activist needs to know.' *Dulwich Labour Party Newsletter.* 'Can help would-be campaign organisers to avoid many of the pitfalls and heartaches ahead.' *Conservative Newsline.* 'Polly Bird is someone that those in authority would be wise not to upset. Her book is a must for all who want to cause authority a headache. . .' *The Chemical Engineer.* 'Highly recommended.' *Care Review.*

144pp illus. 0 7463 0539 7. 1989.

How to Know Your Rights at work
Robert Spicer MA

Workplace law has changed a good deal in recent years and many employees and employers are unaware of even their most basic rights. Written in clear English, this easy-to-follow handbook sets out everyone's rights at work whether in an office, shop, factory or other setting. It outlines the legal framework, the general duties of employers and employees, the legal scope of 'employment', confidential information, references, being a company director, the contract of employment, pay and deductions, hours of work, absences from work, disciplinary procedures, the ACAS code of practice, the meaning of 'gross misconduct', and grievance procedures. It summarises rights, conditions for claims, poor job performance, and the amount of awards. Other chapters explain the law of redundancy, union involvement, what happens on the transfer of a business, guarantee payments, and calculation of redundancy pay. The law relating to sex and racial discrimination is clearly stated and includes a guide to the rights of expectant mothers, disabled people and past offenders. Health and safety at work is also summarised, and the book is complete with a section on going to an industrial tribunal, a list of key statutes, glossary of business law, further reading, useful addresses and index. Frequent use is made of recent court cases to illustrate the text. Robert Spicer MA(Cantab) is a practising barrister, legal editor and author who specialises in employment law. He was Editor of the Case Index of Employment Law (Kluwer) and has taught law at Bristol University and Bristol Polytechnic.

141pp 1 85703 009 5. 1991.

How to Claim State Benefits
Martin Rathfelder
Second Edition

Many claimants are understandably put off by the jungle of rules, regulations and paperwork. This is the *first* popular paperback to be published which explains in clear and simple language exactly what are every citizen's rights and entitlements under the law. Laid out in a quick reference A to Z format it covers a vast range of information in concise form. As featured on *What Would You Do* (Tyne-Tees Television), *Money Box* (BBC Radio 2), *This is Your Right* (Granada Television). Martin Rathfelder is Adviser at the Welfare Rights Unit, Manchester. He has also been Welfare Rights Officer for the Citizens Advice Bureau.

224pp illus. 0 7463 0531 1. 2nd ed. 1988.

How to Know Your Rights: Students
Shirley Meredeen BA

Students today are often faced with a bewildering range of problems, involving for example their colleges, local authorities, landlords, banks, doctors, employers, shopkeepers and government departments such as the DSS. This new student-friendly paperback meets an enormous need for basic information on the academic, financial and social rights of all students in secondary, further or higher education. In plain English it explains students' rights in everything from demos to drug busts, grants and allowances, sexual relationships, discrimination, the parental home, to choice of study, accommodation, appeals and a host of other important and topical matters. The book makes riveting reading (and reference) for students, officials and representatives, student counsellors, tutors and advisers, Citizens' Advice Bureaux, concerned parents and relatives, teachers, lecturers and other education professionals. The book is complete with practical checklists, sample documents, real life examples, and essential contacts and reference. 'Practical and non-judgmental . . . Recommended.' *National Association of Citizens Advice Bureaux.* Shirley Meredeen BA has long experience of counselling and advising students of all backgrounds. Formerly Accommodation Services Officer at the City & East London College, she is now a freelance consultant, trainer and counsellor.

208pp illus. 1 85703 001 X. 1991.

How to Know Your Rights: Teachers
Neil Adams BA

Amid so much educational upheaval many teachers are unsure of how they stand in relation to the school, the head teachers, the governors and the local authority. What exactly is their legal position? What about staffing levels and redundancy? Or rates of pay? What hours of work, or duties, can they be forced to accept? In the wake of the recent Education Reform Acts, this new book meets an urgent need for a clear statement as to where teachers stand from a professional and legal point of view. In plain English it clarifies such vital matters as recruitment procedures, the legal basis of terms and conditions of service, grievance and disciplinary procedures, dismissal of teachers, union membership, sexual, racial and other discrimination, absences from duty, negligence, the concept of in loco parentis and numerous other sensitive and timely matters. Complete with checklists, sample documents and essential reference information. Neil Adams is a specialist in the field of Education Law. The author of the earlier text *Law and Teachers Today,* he lectures regularly on the subject at several Universities, Management Centres, Colleges and Teachers' Centres. A secondary Head of 26 years' standing, he is also an Open University Tutor in Education management.

144pp illus. 1 85703 002 8. 1991.

How to Know Your Rights: Patients
John Frain MB ChB

This book meets an important need for basic information on the rights of patients using Britain's health services. For example can you choose your own doctor? Can you insist on a second opinion? What about hospital waiting lists or access to expensive treatments? Are a young person's health records confidential? In plain language this book spells out exactly where patients and relatives stand in such matters as visits to doctors, clinics and hospitals, confidentiality, abortions, AIDS/HIV, consent to treatment, and rights to treatment, the right to information and records, terminal care, organ donation, medical negligence, complaints and compensation, and many other key topics. John Frain MB ChB studied medicine at Bristol University, and his interests span both clinical and academic medicine. Outside medicine he is actively involved in his local community and his interests include football, history and hill walking.

144pp illus. 1 85703 010 0. 1991.

How to Use a Library
Elizabeth King MA ALA

This user-friendly book will be a boon for students, teachers and others needing the most from their library as a resource centre. *Contents:* Introduction, 1 Libraries are for you, 2 Your information supermarket, 3 Using libraries for study, 4 Using books for reference, 5 Using libraries for research, 6 Other resource centres, 7 Special library services, 8 The information revolution, 9 A typical librarian's day, 10 Some important specialist libraries in Britain, Useful addresses, Glossary of terms, Index. 'The recommended purchase.' *The School Librarian.* Elizabeth King MA ALA is a past Chairman of the School Library Association and a member of the Library Association Joint Board for School Library Studies.

96pp illus. 0 7463 0317 3. Reprinted 1990.